Waging Prophetic Warfa
ject of spiritual warfare
heartedly agree with author Jennifer LeClaire's statement early on that the church has moved from "peacetime Christianity to wartime Christianity." The darkness is darker and the challenges more challenging. Believers globally are being belittled, berated, beaten, and even beheaded for the cause of Christ. It's no longer business as usual. You simply need this book. Warfare at a prophetic level is warring from the very throne room of the Lord, as the Lord Himself wars through the lips of His praying people. To equip believers for this level of intercession, LeClaire sets forth powerful and practical insights for engaging in entirely new dimensions of spiritual warfare on a prophetic level.

—Dick Eastman
International President,
Every Home for Christ

In *Waging Prophetic Warfare*, Jennifer LeClaire encourages and rallies the troops of prophetic intercessors who have been in the fights of the past seasons and grown weary or broken rank due to disappointment, setbacks, and outright wounds from battle. Jennifer gives insight into operating in intercession from a place of wisdom and authority. *Waging Prophetic Warfare* reminds us that, first and foremost, we must discern what the Lord is doing and release it through the many spiritual weapons the Lord has equipped us with for victory—from victory.

—Dr. Ché Ahn
Founding Pastor, HRock Church,
Pasadena, California
President, Harvest International Ministry
International Chancellor,
Wagner Leadership Institute

In this season of heightened warfare, it's time for the spiritual warfare camp and the prophetic ministry camp to merge. It's time for believers to tap into prophetic insights in the face of enemy attacks. In *Waging Prophetic Warfare*, Jennifer LeClaire expertly marries prophecy and spiritual warfare in a way that inspires believers to take a fresh look at the battleground. As a battle-tested prophetic voice and a spiritual warrior, Jennifer equips you to win battles against old enemies and new adversaries.

—Ryan LeStrange
Ryan LeStrange Ministries
Cofounder, AwakeningTV.com
President, New Breed Revival Network

A few decades ago a revolution concerning spiritual warfare, binding the strong man, and loosing divine revelation for breakthroughs against the powers of darkness was germinating. The body of Christ began to be equipped with fresh new biblical understanding, and those who applied the new understanding saw great breakthroughs. Jennifer LeClaire has once again given us another piece to the revolution through her anointed pen and prophetic wisdom. For those who are practitioners of prayer this book can build further dimensions of understanding and grace to carry forward the fullness of this revolution.

—Lou Engle

Cynthia Patton
2017

WAGING PROPHETIC WARFARE

Jennifer LeClaire

Waging Prophetic Warfare

Most Charisma House Book Group products are available at special quantity discounts for bulk purchase for sales promotions, premiums, fund-raising, and educational needs. For details, write Charisma House Book Group, 600 Rinehart Road, Lake Mary, Florida 32746, or telephone (407) 333-0600.

Waging Prophetic Warfare by Jennifer LeClaire
Published by Charisma House
Charisma Media/Charisma House Book Group
600 Rinehart Road
Lake Mary, Florida 32746
www.charismahouse.com

Cover design by Vincent Pirozzi
Design Director: Justin Evans

Visit the author's website at www.JenniferLeClaire.org.

Library of Congress Cataloging-in-Publication Data:
Names: LeClaire, Jennifer (Jennifer L.), author.
Title: Waging prophetic warfare / by Jennifer LeClaire.
Description: Lake Mary, Florida : Charisma House, 2016. | Includes bibliographical references and index.
Identifiers: LCCN 2016032356| ISBN 9781629987262 (trade paper : alk. paper) |
ISBN 9781629987279 (ebook)
Subjects: LCSH: Spiritual warfare.
Classification: LCC BV4509.5 .L4435 2016 | DDC 235/.4--dc23
LC record available at https://lccn.loc.gov/2016032356

16 17 18 19 20 — 9 8 7 6 5 4 3 2
Printed in the United States of America

This book is dedicated to the prophetic warriors who won't quit, the prophetic intercessors who press in, the dreamers and visionaries who gather clues, the praise and worshippers who bring down the glory, the travailing handmaidens who groan too deep for words, the spiritual mappers, the prayer walkers, and others who are waging war against principalities, powers, and every other evil force!

CONTENTS

I appreciate Tessie DeVore, who understands how fierce the battle is and inspires me to fight. I am appreciative of the editing and marketing teams who make me look good and help spread the word. And I'm thankful for my daughter, who is a continual source of encouragement to my heart.

FOREWORD

IN 1990, UNDER the leadership of Peter Wagner and a few others (myself included), the Spiritual Warfare Network was formed to begin the process of equipping the body of Christ with the wisdom and insight for biblically waging spiritual warfare on all levels.

Up to this point there was little to no teaching or resources on this subject. Several of us in the group began writing books to meet this need, including John Dawson's *Taking Our Cities for God*, Ed Silvoso's *That None Should Perish*, and my own book, *Possessing the Gates of the Enemy.*

Little did we know that these books, along with others birthed from that network, were laying the foundation for a movement that would become worldwide in scope.

Still, every generation needs to add fresh revelation, even revisiting and reexamining the teachings that have gone before, and Jennifer LeClaire has done just that in the book you are holding now.

Many of us who pioneered the teachings of spiritual warfare have observed that there is a great need for these topics to be addressed again as they still do not seem to be widely understood in the body of Christ, even being improperly used or neglected. With that knowledge I grew increasingly excited as I read this manuscript. Jennifer is being used to rally the troops once more!

Jennifer LeClaire is a woman of great courage, making a mark in the field of journalism through her work with *Charisma* magazine and in the prayer movement through her personal ministry.

Contained in the pages of this book are life-changing principles. While the topics of prophetic and spiritual warfare can be controversial, for those of us who are practitioners, there is no doubt that what Jennifer writes about here truly works—both theologically and from the practical fruit we have seen through our prayers.

Jennifer's writing style is interesting and practical. If you are new to the concepts of the prophetic and spiritual warfare, this book will give you a firm foundation and grasp of the subjects as well as equip you to apply the principles to your everyday life.

For those who are more seasoned in these areas, *Waging Prophetic Warfare* will sharpen your understanding and provide you with effective materials to use for training others.

Some of you might be feeling like wounded warriors, or be just plain burned out. I encourage you to read this book and allow the Holy Spirit to heal you, energize you, and get you ready to lace up your spiritual combat boots once again!

All of us need to take our place on the wall for our families, cities, and nations. Dive into these pages, and you will be fully equipped for battle!

—Cindy Jacobs
Generals International
Dallas, Texas

Chapter 1

CALLING ALL PROPHETIC WARRIORS

You have probably noticed that spiritual warfare has increased—and is increasing in the last days. It doesn't take a prophet to discern the raging culture wars, the bold rise of principalities like Jezebel, or the spirit of the world that has settled into a front row seat in far too many churches. Whether we like it or not, we are in a war.

Indeed, passive Christianity is no longer an option for those who want to live victorious lives, especially in this world where antichrist agendas are pushing all things of Jesus out of the public square and sexual immorality is celebrated rather than mourned. We have moved from peacetime Christianity to wartime Christianity. Of course, we are not wrestling against flesh and blood but against principalities, powers, rulers of the darkness of this world, and spiritual forces of evil (Eph. 6:12). Although the enemy is unseen, it is very real.

Whether you are new to spiritual warfare or you're an expert warrior, the days in which we live demand full engagement in the battle. We do not have the luxury of retreating and hoping the darkness will not overtake us. There is no cease-fire in the spirit. The devil will not back off and call a truce if we lay our weapons down and take off our armor. Quite the opposite; if we give up the fight, we essentially surrender to the evil forces that are warring against our minds, our bodies, our families, our finances, and the fullness of our destinies. But we are not going to do that!

Here is the problem: many believers are finding that the spiritual warfare tactics they have relied on in the past are less effective—or not effective at all—in forcing the devil to flee. Yet I know that James 4:7 is true: "Therefore submit yourselves to God. Resist the devil, and he will flee from you." Sometimes it feels like I am submitting and resisting with everything in me, yet stubborn devils refuse to obey the Word of God. At times I have wondered if there is a line of demons in formation waiting to step up and take their best shot when one is forced to flee in the name of Jesus. If so, that means we have to live a submitted-resisting lifestyle to hold back the darkness.

In this chapter, I want to rally the troops—the prophetic warriors. I want to reveal to you the power of the end-times spiritual warfare arsenal. God is calling prophetic warriors—those empowered by His Spirit, flowing in the gifts of the Spirit, walking in the fruits of the Spirit, and enforcing the will of the Spirit—to the front lines. Are you ready for the challenge? I'll guarantee you this: if you will press into this paradigm, you will see even old enemies finally flee.

End-Times Prophetic Insight

The signs of the times are all around us. Some are questioning if we are in the beginning of the Tribulation. Others are sure we're at least at the beginning of sorrows. Still others suggest that some of the trumpets named in the Book of Revelation have already sounded. I don't know about all that, but I do know this: Jesus expects us to discern the signs of the times, and the signs I'm seeing convince me that we're in the end times. Consider Paul the apostle's prophecy:

> Know this: In the last days perilous times will come. Men will be lovers of themselves, lovers of money, boastful, proud, blasphemers, disobedient to parents, unthankful, unholy, without natural affection, trucebreakers, slanderers, unrestrained, fierce, despisers of those who are good, traitors, reckless, conceited, lovers of pleasures more than lovers of God, having a form of godliness, but denying its power. Turn away from such people.
>
> —2 Timothy 3:1–5

Beyond the dying birds, earthquakes, floods, droughts, famines, beached sea lions, blood moons, wars, rumors of wars, rise of false prophets, abounding iniquity, health epidemics such as Ebola and the bird flu, microchip implants, and the like, it is obvious that the love of many has grown cold (Matt. 24:12). Police officers are shooting civilians. Massacres are becoming commonplace. Racists are burning down church buildings. And radical Islam has declared war on most of the human race.

The spiritual war is manifesting in the natural like never before seen in our day. Although we can't pray the end times away, we can rise up in the name of Jesus and wage spiritual war against everything that opposes God's will. Of course, that means we need to discern what the will of the Lord is. And that means we need to tap into the prophetic realm to get supernatural intelligence directly from the Spirit of God. God is calling prophetic spiritual warriors to the front lines.

Now is the time to shed some new light on Joel's prophecy about the last days. For decades we have shared it and declared it, but until now I hadn't seen beyond the surface level of the prophecy:

> And it will be that, afterwards, I will pour out My Spirit on all flesh; then your sons and your daughters will

> prophesy, your old men will dream dreams, and your young men will see visions. Even on the menservants and maidservants in those days I will pour out My Spirit. Then I will work wonders in the heavens and the earth—blood and fire and columns of smoke.
>
> —Joel 2:28–30

I believe those prophetic manifestations are part of the end-times prophetic warfare arsenal. Many have pulled back from the battle lines—and even broken rank—because of wounds sustained in battle. But God is raising up a new breed of prophetic warriors—Special Forces—who will march in tandem with the Holy Spirit and see victories. The key to triumph is to follow the Holy Spirit's battle plan and timing.

Tapping Into New Spiritual Warfare Technologies

If you have moved in spiritual warfare circles for any length of time, you will be among the first to understand that "the weapons of our warfare are not carnal, but mighty through God to the pulling down of strongholds" (2 Cor. 10:4). God has given us mighty weapons to pull down strongholds over our lives, our families, and our cities, but sometimes we need new technologies for the battle. With an onslaught of principalities and powers coming against Christians in this hour, we have to do more than sharpen our sword. We need to explore new weapons.

Indeed, the Holy Spirit revealed to me there are spiritual warfare technologies we need to tap into in the last days. This revelation was unlocked while I was on an intercessory prayer call for a spiritual warfare conference. As one of the intercessors was sharing the revelation about the new weapons, the Holy Spirit started talking to me about spiritual warfare technologies. That didn't make much sense to my natural mind because I associate technologies with my computer, my iPhone, or my Kindle e-book reader, but it made strategic sense after I searched it out.

After I heard these words, I quickly looked up the word *technology* in *Merriam-Webster* to try to gain more insight into what Holy Spirit was showing me. The definitions were eye-opening and relevant to all spiritual warriors—especially those who are not seeing the victories they are assured in Christ's name. One definition of technology is "the practical application of knowledge especially in a particular area"; another is "a capability given by the practical application of knowledge."[1]

Let's break that down for a minute. What knowledge do we have that we can use in spiritual battle? First and foremost, we have the Bible, the Word of God, which itself is the "sword of the Spirit" (Eph. 6:17). Jesus answered the devil with the Word of God when He was tempted in the wilderness, and that is always a good first step. But sometimes you need a *rhema* word—a right now spoken word—in the midst of the battle. In chapter 7, we will take a closer look at the power of prophetic declaration, decrees, and proclamations.

Many of us also have prophetic words, dreams, visions, words of knowledge, discerning of spirits, or some other prophetic insight that helps us in battle. In chapter 5, we will explore prophetic dreams that unlock spiritual warfare strategies. Chapter 6 will reveal the spiritual warfare tactics found in prophetic visions, and chapter 9 will delve into waging war with prophetic words.

Here's the rub: We may have the knowledge we need. We may have the revelation about what spirits are operating in the heavenlies. We may see clearly what spirit is attacking our pastor. We may have no doubt about how the enemy is working to hinder God's will on the earth in a particular situation. Indeed, often we have biblical knowledge and even the prophetic insight. What is sometimes lacking is the practical application of that knowledge in the area or God-defying circumstance we are battling.

What we need, then, are spiritual warfare technologies rooted in wisdom. Thank God for James 1:5: "If any of you lacks wisdom, let him ask of God, who gives to all men liberally and without criticism, and it will be given to him." God gives us the weapons of warfare and the wisdom to apply them.

Preparing for Spiritual Battle

I am no stranger to warfare. If you have read my books *Jezebel's Puppets: Exposing the Agenda of False Prophets* or *Satan's Deadly Trio: Defeating the Deceptions of Jezebel, Religion and Witchcraft*, you know that I've walked through fields full of land mines. I've walked through the fire. I've been in the lion's den. I've walked through the waters, through the valleys, and through the wilderness.

Indeed, I have gone toe to toe with Jezebel, endured the religious spirit's accusations, resisted witchcraft's mind traffic, stood up to antichrist spirits, and otherwise prevailed—survived and thrived—despite the devil's attacks against me. I give God the glory, because I felt overwhelmed more than I care to admit. I overreacted and made rash decisions more than I'd like you to know. I wanted to give up more times than I can count. But I'm still standing. Through it all, I have gained wisdom—but I am always looking to gain more.

There is one thing I have been praying for more and more lately. I am convinced that if we would pray more for this one thing, we would make better use of our time, live happier lives, see more answers to our prayers, and ultimately post more battle victories instead of walking in defeat. What is this one thing? Wisdom.

I believe if we pray more for spiritual wisdom—even if it means praying less for natural needs—we will receive more wisdom and our natural needs will be more than met. More importantly, in the context of our prophetic warfare strategies, we will have less trouble with the wicked one. We need wisdom before we enter the battle, wisdom during the battle, and wisdom in dealing with the spoils of battle. We need to crave God's wisdom and refuse to tap into the world's wisdom. Consider James's words:

> Who is wise and understanding among you? Let him show his works by his good life in the meekness of wisdom. But if you have bitter envying and strife in your hearts, do not boast and do not lie against the truth. This wisdom descends not from above, but is earthly, unspiritual, and devilish. For where there is envying and strife, there is confusion and every evil work. But the wisdom that is from above is first pure, then peaceable, gentle, open to reason, full of mercy and good fruits, without partiality, and without hypocrisy. And the fruit of righteousness is sown in peace by those who make peace.
>
> —James 3:13–18

We could all take a hint from James—and from Solomon. You know the story. The Lord appeared to Solomon in a dream and made this invitation: "Ask what you want from Me" (1 Kings 3:5). Can you imagine the Lord coming to you in a prophetic dream and making such an invitation? What would you ask God for if you could ask and assuredly receive anything? Carnal Christians would ask for a spouse or a new car or a million bucks.

On the other hand, spiritually-minded Christians would do what Solomon did. Solomon had enough wisdom to ask for the principal thing: wisdom. Solomon replied to God's invitation with these words: "Give Your servant therefore an understanding heart to judge Your people, that I may discern between good and bad" (1 Kings 3:9). Other translations use the word *evil.* Discerning between good and evil is half the battle in spiritual warfare, especially in an age where some prophets and pastors are calling "evil good, and good evil" (Isa. 5:20).

Solomon's quest for wisdom made God happy. Let's see how He responded:

> Because you have asked this and have not asked for yourself long life or riches or the lives of your enemies, but have asked for yourself wisdom so that you may have discernment in judging, I now do according to your words. I have given you a wise and an understanding heart, so that there has never been anyone like you in the past, and there shall never arise another like you. I have also given you what you have not asked, both riches and honor, so that no kings will compare to you all of your days. If you will walk in My ways, keeping My statutes and My commandments as your father David did, then I will lengthen your days.
>
> —1 Kings 3:11–14

All I can say to that is "wow" and "amen."

Wisdom Helps in Warfare

"God is no respecter of persons" (Acts 10:34). You can receive the wisdom you need to walk according to God's plan for you and to trample on the enemy's assignments against your life. As I mentioned earlier, James made it clear that "If any of you lacks wisdom, let him ask of God, who gives to all liberally and without reproach, and it will be given to him" (James 1:5, NKJV).

The only catch is that you have to ask in faith, without doubting. That's not much of a catch, and it shouldn't be too hard to do. God wants to give you wisdom so you can walk wisely, making the best use of your time, because the days are evil (Eph. 5:15–17). He wants to give you wisdom in the midst of the battle so you can gain the victory—and collect the spoils. He wants to reveal to you spiritual warfare technologies. Wisdom brings joy, and the joy of the Lord is your strength in battle (Neh. 8:10).

Consider Solomon's words:

> Happy is the man who finds wisdom, and the man who gets understanding; for her benefit is more profitable than silver, and her gain than fine gold. She is more precious than rubies, and all the things you may desire are not to be compared with her. Length of days is in her right hand, and in her left hand riches and honor. Her ways are ways of pleasantness, and all her paths are peace. She is a tree of life to those who take hold of her, and happy is everyone who retains her.
>
> —Proverbs 3:13–18

Wisdom begets wisdom. "The ear of the wise seeks knowledge" (Prov. 18:15). The wise man listens to advice (Prov. 12:15). "A man's wisdom makes his face shine" (Eccles. 8:1). By wisdom your house is built (Prov. 24:3). Wise ones are cautious and turn away from evil (Prov. 14:16, NASB). The words of the wise win him favor (Eccles. 10:12). The wise will inherit honor (Prov. 3:35, NASB). Wisdom will keep and guard you if you love it (Prov. 4:5–6). I could go on and on, and encourage you to do a study of the benefits of walking in God's wisdom. You already have authority in the name of Jesus. You already have the whole armor of God. What you need is the wisdom to walk in what you have.

When we receive wisdom, it is important that we acknowledge its source. "The LORD gives wisdom" (Prov. 2:6). We should never be wise in our own eyes (Prov. 3:7), but we should humbly pray for wisdom more and more. So these are my prayers. I pray like Solomon, who said, "Give Your servant therefore an understanding heart to judge Your people, that I may discern between good and bad" (1 Kings 3:9).

And I pray like Paul, who asked:

> So that the God of our Lord Jesus Christ, the Father of glory, may give you the Spirit of wisdom and revelation in the knowledge of Him, that the eyes of your understanding may be enlightened, that you may know what is the hope of His calling and what are the riches of the glory of His inheritance among the saints, and what is the surpassing greatness of His power toward us who believe, according to the working of His mighty power, which He performed in Christ when He raised Him from the dead and seated Him at His own right hand in the heavenly places, far above all principalities, and power, and might, and dominion, and every name that is named, not only in this age but also in that which is to come.
>
> —EPHESIANS 1:17–21

And I pray the Lord would give you wisdom and discernment too. Amen.

GOD'S SPECIAL FORCES

Now, a second definition of technology is "a manner of accomplishing a task especially using technical processes, methods, or knowledge" or "the specialized aspects of a particular field of endeavor."[2] Let's break that down from a spiritual angle. When we enter into battle in these last days, we may need to go about things a little differently than we have in the past. The methods we have always used might not bear the same victorious fruit.

This definition also struck me because one of the other intercessors on the call had a word about specialists—like Special Forces (SF) or Green Berets. The US Army Special Forces is described as "a unique, Special Warfare organization filled with trained, seasoned, professional Soldiers...Due to their extensive training, they are among the most versatile Special Operations Soldiers in the world. SF missions often require rapid and discreet responses to unique situations throughout the world. At the tip of the spear in our nation's defense, SF Soldiers are generally the first on the ground or already at a crisis location as trouble emerges. Special Forces Soldiers are unquestioned experts in unconventional warfare."[3]

There are different levels of spiritual warfare. A baby Christian doesn't have the training or spiritual warfare technologies to battle at the same heights as a seasoned warrior. God needs specialists in this hour to work as part of spiritual warfare teams to dismantle the enemy's plans over churches, cities, and regions. I believe He is calling you as a specialist.

During the prayer call I mentioned, the Holy Spirit also showed me that we already possess every weapon we need for battle but we sometimes don't know we have them. He showed me that the fruit of the Spirit manifested can be a weapon against the enemy: love, joy, peace, patience, gentleness, goodness, faith, meekness, and self-control (Gal. 5:22–23). It drives the devil crazy when you walk in love or remain at peace when he is working through people or circumstances to throw you off balance. It's one way we submit ourselves to God, resist the devil, and watch him flee (James 4:7).

Here is the bottom line: many of us have become accustomed to waging spiritual warfare in a certain way and have seen strong results, but in this new season we may need to seek new spiritual warfare technologies—new practical applications of knowledge and an awareness of the breadth of the weapons we actually possess. Then we will have the "capability given by the practical application of knowledge."[4] We will have the right weapon applied in the right way at the right time. That is what we will dive into in the chapters ahead. These are not necessarily brand-new revelations, but collectively they offer a fresh look—and prophetic insight—into waging war in the end times.

Calling Back the Wounded Warriors

We are in a season of war, and we need all the spiritual warriors in formation. But the Holy Spirit has shown me that some have broken rank. During the same prayer call I mentioned earlier, the prayer leader asked if anyone had anything else to share. I hesitated because so much had already been unpacked during the call, but I kept hearing the Holy Spirit saying, "Breaking rank."

When the prayer leader asked me specifically if I had something to share, I decided I'd better be obedient to the Holy Spirit's prompting. When I began sharing how the Holy Spirit told me many have broken rank, prophecy started flowing:

> Many are breaking rank. They are sitting on the sidelines when they should be waging warfare. Some of them were wounded in battle. Some of them were even hit with friendly fire. They are tending to their wounds, and they are out of formation.
>
> When they hear this message about new weapons for a new season—about spiritual warfare technologies—their spirits will bear witness. They will get a new revelation that will bring healing and strengthen them for the battle. They will pick up their weapons and run to

the battle line—and they will even call others forth who have been hanging back.

Now, I don't believe the Holy Spirit was talking about those who are compromising the gospel—the hyper-grace adherents, the gay-affirming theologians, and the rest. I believe He was speaking specifically about those spiritual warriors who have withdrawn from battle. They have broken ranks for whatever reason. It may be hurts and wounds, fear, flat out rebellion, or something else.

Getting Back in Formation

The American Heritage Dictionary of Idioms defines *break ranks* this way: "fall out of line or into disorder; also, fail to conform, deviate."[5] *The Cambridge Dictionary of American Idioms* explains the military meaning: "to walk away from a straight row in which you and other soldiers have been standing."[6]

In a military sense, ranks are the members of an armed service—the enlisted personnel, not the officers. In some cases the ranks have been wounded by the officers leading them, sending them into a battle they weren't trained well enough to fight or throwing them in the line of fire to protect themselves. In other cases, ranks have wounded themselves by not following orders or have been hit with friendly fire from others in God's army who were careless or disobedient.

Whatever the case, it's time to get back into formation. David's mighty men did not break rank. Gideon's army did not break rank. As soldiers in the army of the Lord, we must not break rank. We must remain loyal to the Captain of Hosts.

If you have been wounded by friendly fire in battle, forgive those who hurt you and let the Lord heal you so you can take your rightful place. God needs you at your post. If you have been oppressed by the enemy and are fearful of returning to the front lines, take counsel with wise warriors who can take authority in prayer over the enemy's assignment against your life, help you discover new spiritual warfare technologies, and stand with you in warfare. God needs you at your post.

Finally, if you have rebelled against God, repent, receive forgiveness, and pick up your weapons again. You don't disengage from the war just because you choose not to fight. The battle against you will continue to rage. Get back in formation. God needs you at your post, and He has great spoils of war for you to collect.

CHAPTER 2

WIELDING THE WEAPONS OF OUR WARFARE

BEFORE YOU CAN enter the Special Forces, you need to go through boot camp. You can't expertly shoot a gun until you know how it operates—and how to use it safely. Basic training is essential to gain the wisdom you will need to wield the weapons of warfare expertly. As I always say, the strength is in the fundamentals.

You could relate this to basketball—or just about any sport, I suppose. I'm a big basketball fan. Although I don't have much time these days to turn on a game, I still appreciate warriors like Larry Bird, Michael Jordan, and, more recently, Tim Duncan. Duncan is also known as "Mr. Fundamental" because he has mastered the fundamentals of the game.

The six-foot-eleven, 250-pound Duncan might not be as spectacular as LeBron James, but his precision is undeniable. He's spent his whole career wearing a San Antonio Spurs jersey. During that time the power forward has earned five NBA championships, was the NBA MVP twice, was the NBA Finals MVP three times, and is the only player to ever land on both the All-NBA and All-Defensive Teams in each of his first thirteen seasons.

How did he achieve such great success in the sports battlefield called the NBA? Talent, yes, but most point to his mastery of the fundamentals. Early on in my spiritual warfare training, I had limited revelation and a limited arsenal. I was lacking in solid spiritual warfare fundamentals. I thought everything was Jezebel or witchcraft. All I knew how to do was bind and plead the blood. I didn't have a full revelation of the believer's authority, and my arms grew weary holding up a shield of faith that had holes in it.

So before we jump into the many prophetic warfare strategies outlined in this book, let's make sure we've got our fundamentals down. You sure don't want to build your spiritual warfare wisdom on a faulty foundation. Armed with the revelations in this chapter, you will be well equipped to bring out old and new treasures of spiritual warfare revelation (Matt. 13:52).

Who Are We Really Fighting

Paul told his spiritual son Timothy to "fight the good fight of faith" (1 Tim. 6:12). Although there are true physical threats that manifest, we are usually fighting a battle against our mind. But who is waging war against our souls? As Paul explains, "We wrestle not against flesh and blood, but against principalities, against powers, against the rulers of the darkness of this world, against spiritual wickedness in high places" (Eph. 6:12, KJV).

Let's break this down in the Greek. First, notice that we are wrestling. We are not wrestling people; we are wrestling the enemy's unseen Special Forces assigned to derail our destiny. According to *The KJV New Testament Greek Lexicon*, the Greek word translated as *wrestling* in this verse refers to "a contest between two in which each endeavors to throw the other, and which is decided when the victor is able to hold his opponent down with his hand upon his neck."[1]

The devil wants to put you in a stranglehold. In the wrestling world, a stranglehold is an illegal hold that chokes the opponent. *Merriam-Webster* calls it a "force or influence that chokes or suppresses freedom of movement or expression."[2] If the wrestler doesn't break free from the stranglehold, the lack of blood or air can cause him to black out.

Translating this to our spiritual realities, the enemy wants to choke the Word of God out of your mouth so you can't wield the sword of the Spirit or pray. He wants to choke your revelation of who you are in Christ and your authority over him. The enemy wants to counter the work of the blood of Jesus and the Holy Spirit in your life so you will sideline yourself.

We see this concept of holding your opponent down with pressure upon his neck in Joshua 10. Joshua led the Israelites into battle against five Amorite kings. The kings hid in the cave at Makkedah, and Joshua, with his prophetic wisdom, instructed some men in his army to "roll large stones over the mouth of the cave, and station men to stand guard over it" (Josh. 10:18). The Israelites went on to defeat the Amorite soldiers (representative of garden-variety harassing demons), but Joshua still wanted to deal with the leaders (representative of principalities and powers and rulers of darkness). Look what happened next:

> Joshua said, "Open the mouth of the cave, and bring out to me those five kings from the cave." They did this, and they brought out those five kings from the cave: the kings of Jerusalem, Hebron, Jarmuth, Lachish, and Eglon. When they brought out those five kings to Joshua, he called out to all the men of Israel and the army commanders, "Come here and place your feet on the necks of these kings." So they came near and placed their feet on their necks. Then Joshua said to them, "Do not be afraid or dismayed. Be strong and courageous! For this is what the LORD will do to all your enemies against whom you fight." After that, Joshua struck them down, killed them, and hung them on five trees.
>
> —JOSHUA 10:22–26

Joshua won the wrestling match. Although his enemies had a foot instead of a hand upon their necks, it is the same principle. David also used this principle. He once said, "You gave me the necks of my enemies, and I destroyed those who hate me" (Ps. 18:40). Again, we are not wrestling against flesh and blood kings. Our enemies are purely spiritual, though sometimes even the most well-intentioned believer can serve as a vessel of enemy attack.

Don't Play Patty-Cake with Principalities

When I was a kid, we played a clapping game called patty-cake. Maybe you played it too. It went like this: "Patty-cake, patty-cake, baker's man/ Bake me a cake as fast as you can/ Roll it, pat it, mark it with a B/ Put it in the oven for baby and me." It was great fun. But we don't play patty-cake with the principalities and powers. When you enter into spiritual warfare, you have to put aside childish things. You don't play games with the devil. He wants to kill you.

Paul told the church at Corinth: "When I was a child, I spoke as a child, I understood as a child, and I thought as a child. But when I became a man, I put away childish things" (1 Cor. 13:11). Childish things—things carnal Christians hold on to such as envy, strife, pet sins, and the like—open the door for the enemy. Again, you can't play games with the devil in your flesh without risking a severe beatdown. You need to set aside childish things if you want to execute prophetic warfare strategies.

According to *The KJV New Testament Greek Lexicon*, the word *principality* comes from the Greek word *arche*. In Ephesians 6:12, the word *principalities* refers to "the first place, principality, rule, magistracy" and speaks of "angels and demons."[3] *Vine's Expository Dictionary* reveals that it is used of "supramundane beings who exercise rule."[4] These are high-level demons—so high-level, in fact, that an angel needed help from an archangel to break through. Remember Daniel's encounter:

> But then a hand touched me, which set me on my knees and on the palms of my hands. He said to me, "O Daniel, a man greatly beloved, understand the words that I speak to you, and stand upright, for I have been sent to you now." And when he had spoken this word to me, I stood trembling. Then he said to me, "Do not be afraid, Daniel. For from the first day that you set your heart to understand this and to humble yourself before your God, your words were heard, and I have come because of your words. But the prince of the kingdom of Persia withstood me for twenty-one days. So Michael, one of the chief princes, came to help me, for I had been left there with the kings of Persia."
>
> —Daniel 10:10–13

The Greek word for *powers* in Ephesians 6:12 (*exousia*) refers to "the leading and more powerful among created beings superior to main, spiritual potentates."[5] Moving down the hierarchy, a *ruler*, which comes from the Greek word *kosmokrator*, means "lord of the world, prince of this age,"[6] and *wickedness*, from the Greek word *poneria,* means "depravity, iniquity, wickedness; malice; evil purposes and desires."[7]

See what we're up against? If the angel needed help from another angel to get around this principality, how much more do we need help from angels and the Holy Spirit? We will talk more about partnering with angelic messengers in warfare in chapter 12. The point is, we cannot battle our spiritual enemies in our own strength, but when we discover the fundamentals of spiritual warfare and execute prophetic strategies, the Goliaths in our life will fall.

Our Weapons Are Not Carnal

For decades we have been taught 2 Corinthians 10:4. In fact, most of us have it memorized: "For the weapons of our warfare are not carnal, but mighty through God to the pulling down of strongholds." Still, many in the body of Christ are relying on carnal weapons—even works of the flesh—to battle against perceived human enemies. It's no wonder so many Christians are walking around in defeat. The good news is that we can patch this crack in our foundation.

We will start by looking at some Greek words in 2 Corinthians 10:4. The Greek word for *weapons* in this scripture is *hoplon*, which in this context means "arms used in warfare, weapons."[8] *Warfare* comes from the word *strateia*, meaning "an expedition, campaign, military service, warfare."[9]

Metaphorically, the lexicon suggests, "Paul likens his contest with the difficulties that oppose him in the discharge of his apostolic duties to a warfare."[10] In other words, warfare can manifest in many different ways. Warfare can come against your body, your family, or your finances; warfare can cause delays and detours; warfare can cause people whom you thought were on your side to betray you. You get the idea.

Now I want to spend a minute on the word *carnal*, which comes from the Greek word *sarkikos*. It means "fleshly, carnal; having the nature of flesh, i.e. under the control of the animal appetites; governed by mere human nature not by the Spirit of God; having its seat in the animal nature or aroused by the animal nature; human: with the included idea of depravity; pertaining to the flesh," according to *The KJV New Testament Greek Lexicon.*[11]

I see a lot of spiritual Christians waging carnal warfare against principalities and powers. When there are problems in the church, carnal warriors engage in envy, strife, and divisions. (See 1 Corinthians 3:1–4.) When there are relationship problems, carnal warriors have a tendency to tap into the fleshly work of witchcraft and give their opponents the silent treatment to teach them a lesson. When there are financial problems, carnal warriors stop tithing or giving offerings. When there are health problems, carnal warriors rely on the doctor more than the Word of God. There's nothing wrong with doctors, but we need to hit it from both sides. The Lord told Jeremiah, "Cursed is the man who…makes flesh his strength" (Jer. 17:5).

If we try to wage spiritual warfare with a carnal mind, we won't like the outcome. We cannot be led forth into battle by the Spirit of God—discerning prophetic warfare strategies that are mighty in God to the pulling down of strongholds—when we are walking in the flesh. We won't bless those who curse us when we're waging carnal warfare. We won't be peacemakers when we're waging carnal warfare. We certainly won't walk in love when we're waging carnal warfare.

If you want to tap into prophetic warfare strategies, you need to walk in the Spirit. It's like Paul told the Galatians: "I say then, walk in the Spirit, and you shall not fulfill the lust of the flesh. For the flesh lusts against the Spirit, and the Spirit against the flesh" (Gal. 5:16–17). When you wage carnal warfare, you are setting yourself up for a lost battle. Sure, you still win the war in the end because you are in Christ, but the road to your ultimate victory will be paved with bumps and bruises. Consider what Paul told the church in Rome:

> For those who live according to the flesh set their minds on the things of the flesh, but those who live according to the Spirit, the things of the Spirit. To be carnally minded is death, but to be spiritually minded is life and peace, for the carnal mind is hostile toward God, for it is

> not subject to the law of God, nor indeed can it be, and those who are in the flesh cannot please God.
>
> —Romans 8:5–8

Our Weapons Are Mighty

Let's take a look at 2 Corinthians 10:4 again: "For the weapons of our warfare are not carnal, but mighty through God to the pulling down of strongholds." Our weapons are not carnal; they are mighty. The Greek word for *mighty* in this verse is *dunatos*. It means "able, powerful, mighty, strong; mighty in wealth and influence; strong in soul; to bear calamities and trials with fortitude and patience; strong in Christian virtue; to be able (to do something); mighty, excelling in something; having power for something."[12]

Wow. I don't know about you, but I will take the mighty weapons over the carnal weapons every time. It's when we use the mighty weapons that we are "more than conquerors" in battle (Rom. 8:37). It's when we use the mighty weapons that we can walk practically in the reality that greater is He who is in us than he who is in the world (1 John 4:4). It's when we use the mighty weapons that God leads us into triumph in Christ (2 Cor. 2:14). See the contrast between this and carnal weapons? Again, I will take the mighty weapons over the carnal any day.

That means you don't need to scream at the devil to make him bow. Some spiritual warriors equate volume with power; they scream at the devil as if he's deaf. But the devil is not deaf, and screaming doesn't convince him to bow. When results elude them, some spiritual warriors grow louder and begin to moan and groan and make threats against the enemy they don't have the authority to enforce. I actually was trained in spiritual warfare in a church that hollered and wailed at the enemy in this manner with few results.

I am not against fervent spiritual warfare prayer or even getting loud. What I'm saying is the yelling that comes from frustration or out of a wrong mind-set that louder is more powerful is not fruitful. One of my mentors once said spiritual warfare skills aren't taught; they are caught. There is some truth to that. I believe some spiritual warriors scream and holler and make threats against the devil because that's what they have seen modeled. But that's not what the Bible models. That's not how Jesus did it.

So as you engage in spiritual warfare, don't get frustrated and abandon the fruit of self-control. Don't start acting like the devil! Remember, our weapons are mighty in God. In order to wield our weapons rightly, we need to know who we are in Christ, what our weapons are, and how to use them. There are entire books written on the authority of the believer, who we are in Christ, and all of our weapons; we'll look at some of that in the next section. But remember what Jesus said and rejoice: "Look, I give you authority to trample on serpents and scorpions, and over all the power of the enemy. And nothing shall by any means hurt you" (Luke 10:19).

Putting On Your Prophetic Armor

Before you can wage prophetic warfare, you need to put on your prophetic armor. It is one of those fundamentals I told you about earlier in the chapter. Who in their right mind would run to the battle line without the right equipment? Paul describes this spiritual outfit in Ephesians 6:14–17:

> Stand therefore, having your waist girded with truth, having put on the breastplate of righteousness, having your feet fitted with the readiness of the gospel of peace, and above all, taking the shield of faith, with which you will be able to extinguish all the fiery arrows of the evil

> one. Take the helmet of salvation and the sword of the Spirit, which is the word of God.

Jesus paid the price for our prophetic armor, but it's up to us to put it on. If you neglect to put on the whole armor—if you leave the house without your shoes of peace because you were too busy arguing with your spouse, sister, brother, child, or fill-in-the-blank—then you have left yourself vulnerable to the wicked one. If you disregard any piece of your battle array, you are open to attack.

Think of it this way: each element of your armor works with the others to offer complete protection in the face of spiritual opposition. The very word *armor* suggests an assembly of parts, not a single piece. How can your faith work without the belt of truth? It can't. Hearing the word of truth activates your faith. How can your faith work without the breastplate of righteousness? It can't. If you do not have a revelation of your righteousness coming from Christ, the devil will successfully drag you into the pit of self-condemnation every time you make the slightest mistake. The sword of the Spirit, which is the Word of God, won't work for you if you don't wield it in faith.

Consider the seven sons of Sceva. Sceva was a Jew and a chief of the priests. As such, his sons were educated in the Word of God. They took it upon themselves to try to cast out evil spirits, saying, "We command you to come out in the name of Jesus whom Paul preaches" (Acts 19:13). The only problem was that these seven sons of Sceva didn't have faith in the Word of God made flesh. In other words, they didn't have faith in Jesus and had no basis on which to exercise His authority. They didn't have a relationship with Him. They were not born again. The devils knew they had no authority to use the name. Let's look at the fate of these young men:

> The evil spirit answered, "I know Jesus, and I know Paul, but who are you?" Then the man in whom the evil spirit was jumped on them, overpowered them, and prevailed against them, so that they fled from that house naked and wounded.
>
> —Acts 19:15–16

Now let me ask you this: Do you think these seven sons of Sceva were wearing the armor of God? I submit to you that if they had been, the outcome of this spiritual confrontation would have been much different. But these sons of Sceva didn't even have the helmet of salvation, much less the breastplate of righteousness or the gospel of peace. The good news is that if you are a born-again believer, you have authority. Jesus gave it to you (Luke 10:19–20). Faith in the Lord Jesus Christ, His Word, and His name is what gives you the strength to wield the sword.

What Are Our Mighty Weapons?

Here is one last word before we move into the many prophetic warfare strategies in this book: a strategy is one thing, a tactic is another—but weapons are altogether different. We have an arsenal of mighty weapons at our disposal, and God will use them as we execute prophetic warfare strategies. So what are those mighty weapons?

We already talked about one: the sword of the Spirit, which is the Word of God. The writer of Hebrews explains: "For the word of God is alive, and active, and sharper than any two-edged sword, piercing even to the division of soul and spirit, of joints and marrow, and able to judge the thoughts and intents of the heart" (Heb. 4:12). In other words, the sayings of God, the decrees of God, the mandates of God, the moral precepts of God, the prophecy that comes from God, the teaching of

God, and the reasoning of God—all of these are sharp enough to cut through any assignment of the enemy.

Revelation 12 offers a trio of weapons at our disposal: "They overcame him by the blood of the Lamb and by the word of their testimony, and they loved not their lives unto the death" (Rev. 12:11). Since the battle is largely in the mind, pleading the blood of Jesus over your mind is a mighty weapon. We know there is power in the blood of Jesus to break every bondage. Of course, prayer is a mighty weapon. We can pray that God looses His ministering angels and pray that the Holy Spirit helps us and gives us strategies, wisdom, and strength. We can take authority over the enemy and bind and loose in prayer.

The word of our testimony is the second weapon mentioned in the verse, and it is a mighty one. There are two sides to this coin. One side is this: What is coming out of your mouth? What are you confessing? If you are confessing defeat, you are giving the devil ammunition against you. The other side of the coin is your personal testimony. Remembering and confessing what God has delivered you from—past victories—is a mighty weapon.

The third prong of this scripture is one that many don't consider a weapon: loving not your life even unto death. In other words, trade self-pity for selflessness. Self is a snare on the battlefield. Selflessness is a mighty weapon because it places your mind not on the things of the flesh but on executing God's will and trusting Him to take care of you.

Our mighty weapons are many: the name of Jesus, praise and worship, the knowledge of our covenant with God, submission to authority, the gifts of the Spirit, the fruit of the Spirit, and forgiveness. This is not an exhaustive list, and again, there are entire books written on these aspects of spiritual warfare. The point is that you have the prophetic armor of God and many mighty weapons. You have the spiritual warfare technologies at your disposal. What you need is a revelation of prophetic warfare strategies—and the Spirit-led inspiration to use the right one at the right time. It all starts with the art and science of prophetic intercession, which we will look at in the next chapter.

Chapter 3

THE ART AND SCIENCE OF PROPHETIC INTERCESSION

Prophetic intercession is not a new concept. Nevertheless, different people have different definitions of this type of prayer. As we approach this abstract topic, it is helpful to glean from the generals of intercession while also praying for direct revelation from the Spirit of God and, of course, studying the Word of God.

In doing all of this, I have discovered that there is an art and science to prophetic intercession, and it doesn't always look the same in every setting—but there are some fundamentals on which we can build. Remember, the strength is in the fundamentals. I'm not one to stray beyond the boundaries of the Word of God, and the Holy Spirit isn't either. The fundamentals of prophetic intercession are a springboard to waging prophetic warfare that blindsides the enemy.

Before we explore various perspectives of this type of prayer, let's look at the two sides of this prayer: art and science. I use those terms loosely to express the concept that we are partnering with the Holy Spirit in prophetic intercession. We can't do it without Him, and He won't do it without us. He is praying with us and through us. Put another way, prophetic intercession by its nature suggests that the Holy Spirit is offering us strategic insights as we pray so that we can use the authority we carry in the natural realm to enforce the Father's will on Earth.

When I say that prophetic intercession is an art, I mean that it is a skill that sharpens with experience or observation. Prophetic intercession is both taught and caught. You grow in prophetic intercession by practicing prophetic intercession. Like anything, you master it by doing it. You can't decide to enter prophetic intercession; the Spirit of God must lead you into it. That is where the science, which is essentially the operation of laws, comes in. There are laws in the Spirit that He will help you understand and use to your advantage through prophetic intercession.

What Is Prophetic Intercession?

Understanding prophetic intercession in its most straightforward form means to understand how the prophetic realm meets the intercessory realm. Not all prayer is prophetic. Not all prayer is intercession. Not all intercession is prophetic. Not all intercession is prayer. And you don't have to be a prophet to be prophetic. If you have the Holy Spirit living on the inside of you, then you have a prophetic nature because the Holy Spirit is a prophetic spirit.

One who is prophetic senses spiritually what the Lord—or the enemy—is doing and saying. A prophetic person hears the voice of the Lord or demon spirits that are speaking to people; he discerns the activity of the Holy Spirit and devils; she has inklings, impressions, and unctions about what is about to happen in places and to people; and he often has a burden of the Lord that he may not be able to express in mere words.

Now, the prophetic person will often be miserable if he doesn't connect this spiritual gift to intercession. Intercession is an act or a prayer that pleads a case to God on another's behalf. You pray for yourself; you make intercession for others. Again, not all intercession is prayer by definition; one can intercede in ways that go beyond prayer through mediation, arbitration, negotiation, and the like. But for our purposes, intercession is standing in the gap between a person and God, pleading for someone's needs, such as healing, mercy, financial provision, or some other deficit.

Prophetic intercession, then, is intercession that is rooted in discerning what the Lord is saying and doing or discerning what principalities, powers, rulers of darkness, and spiritual wickedness are present. Prophetic intercession bases prayer and spiritual warfare in the wisdom of God for a specific person, place, or situation. Prophetic intercession by its nature must be grounded by the leading and guiding of the Spirit of God. It can include several gifts of the Spirit, including tongues and interpretation of tongues, prophecy, discerning of spirits, word of wisdom, and word of knowledge.

Prophetic Intercessors in the Bible

In Cindy Jacobs's book *The Voice of God: How God Speaks Personally and Corporately to His Children Today*, she writes:

> Prophetic intercession is the ability to receive an immediate prayer request from God and pray about it in a divinely anointed utterance...Many times, such prayer requests come in the form of prophetic words. The people praying may not realize this at the time and only later find out it was God speaking to them to pray prophetically. At times when I pray like this, it is not so much that God gives me a lengthy prophecy, but a name will come to me while I am praying. I then open my mouth to pray and trust God to fill it with the word of intercession He wants. Yet on other occasions, I will ask the Lord, "How do you want me to pray for this matter?" and He will give me the next instruction.[1]

You can find plenty of prophetic intercessors in the Bible, including Abraham, Moses, Daniel, and of course, Jesus. One of the most touching accounts is in Genesis 18, when the Lord told Abraham He would go down and see if the rumors about Sodom and Gomorrah, two especially perverted cities, were true. Abraham immediately interceded for the cities:

> Then Abraham drew near and said, "Shall You also destroy the righteous with the wicked? What if there are fifty righteous in the city? Shall You also destroy, and not spare the place, for the fifty righteous who are in it? Far be it from You to do such a thing as this, to slay the righteous with the wicked, so that the righteous should be treated like the wicked; far be it from You. Should not the Judge of all the earth do right?"
>
> So the LORD said, "If I find in Sodom fifty righteous within the city, then I will spare the entire place for their sakes."
>
> Then Abraham answered and said, "I who am but dust and ashes have taken it upon myself to speak to the Lord. Suppose there were five less than the fifty righteous. Will You destroy all the city for lack of five?"
>
> And He said, "If I find forty-five there, I will not destroy it."
>
> And he spoke to Him yet again and said, "Suppose there will be forty found there?"
>
> So He said, "I will not do it for the sake of forty."
>
> Then he said to Him, "Let not the Lord be angry, and I will speak. Suppose there will be thirty found there?"
>
> Again He said, "I will not do it if I find thirty there."
>
> He said, "Behold, I have undertaken to speak to the Lord. Suppose twenty are found there?"
>
> He said, "I will not destroy it for the sake of twenty."
>
> Then he said, "Let not the Lord be angry, and I will speak only once more. Suppose ten will be found there?"

> Then He said, "I will not destroy it for the sake of ten."
> So the LORD went His way as soon as He had stopped speaking to Abraham, and Abraham returned to his place.
>
> —GENESIS 18:23–33

What makes this intercession prophetic? Remember part of my definition: prophetic intercession is intercession that is rooted in discerning what the Lord is saying and doing—or discerning what principalities, powers, rulers of darkness, and spiritual wickedness are present. Abraham heard the Lord's heart and engaged in active pleas for mercy, even over these especially sinful cities. Mercy is the heartbeat of a true prophetic intercessor. You can find other examples of prophetic intercessors in Exodus 32:7–14; Daniel 9:1–4, 20–22; Luke 2:36–38; John 17; Acts 9:10–17; and Acts 22:17–21.

PRAYING THE PROMISES BACK TO GOD

James Goll, president of Encounters Network, offers another definition of prophetic intercession: "It is the place where the ministry of the priest and prophet unite."[2] He points to Jeremiah 27:18 as an example in Scripture: "But if they are prophets, and if the word of the LORD is with them, let them now make intercession to the LORD of Hosts, that the vessels which are left in the house of the LORD and in the house of the king of Judah and in Jerusalem not go to Babylon."

Goll explains that prophetic people "do not simply pronounce the word of the Lord only; they pray the promise back to Him!" In this sense, he says, prophetic intercessors "actually give birth to it and bring it into being."[3]

"Prophetic intercession, therefore, paves the way for the fulfillment of the prophetic promise," Goll says. "Prophetic intercession is our conspiring together with God, 'breathing violently' into situations through prayer to bring forth life.

When God's people in community have the spirit of grace and supplication poured out on them (see Zech. 12:10), they share a joint sense of divine possibility and become excited that circumstances are about to change. The old limits and expectations of what God wants to accomplish are radically overturned."[4]

Dutch Sheets, author of *Intercessory Prayer*, offers an all-inclusive definition in the foreword to Barbara Wentroble's book *Prophetic Intercession*:

> Prophetic intercession is not confined to a select group; it is for any and all who hunger to act in the midst of His will...The lack of prophetic intercession creates a blind side that we cannot afford in church leadership, in one-on-one counseling or in citywide evangelism. We need to have vigilance, diligence and humility as we intercede prophetically for pastors, counselors and evangelists.[5]

Recognizing Intercessory Prayer Burdens

One day I was sitting on the edge of a worn-out bed in a foreign city with my head in my hands trying to shake off a flood of disturbing emotions. I knew I couldn't effectively minister until I got to the root of the issue.

"What is wrong with me, Lord? I have absolutely no reason to feel this way. What is going on?" I pled with the Lord to reveal the root. I felt like my world was coming to an end, like there was no hope for a better tomorrow. I felt like quitting and giving up. I started praying in the Spirit and then entered another plea.

"What is happening, Lord?"

This time, He replied. "It's despondency. This is how the people of this city feel. I want you to pray for them."

Merriam-Webster defines *despondent* as "feeling or showing extreme discouragement, dejection, or depression."[6] And that nailed it. That was exactly how I was feeling—only it wasn't me. It was a prayer burden from the Lord.

Of course, that was many years ago. I was reminded of that story after a recent message I posted on Facebook about intercession. It was short and sweet, but it hit a nerve with people who were looking for answers—or reminders—about this spiritual truth. I actually wrote the post after discerning an unusual prayer burden the night before. Here is the post:

> Intercessors, as we move deeper and deeper into the things of God, it's increasingly vital to learn to divide soul from spirit. When the burden of the Lord comes upon you, you may feel the weight of oppression, hear the enemy's accusations, or experience various negative emotions seemingly out of the blue. That's not you! Learn to quickly discern the call to pray against a thing rather than coming up under it.[7]

In other words, we need to discern between the emotions of our soul and the prayer burden of the Lord. I can sit in a church and hear what the devil is saying to other members of the congregation. When I was very young in the Lord, I used to think it was my own thoughts. But I learned that I was hearing into the spirit realm so I could engage in warfare over these people's souls—to push back darkness so the enemy could not steal out of their hearts the word they were hearing before it even took root. Many times I feel disturbed in my spirit without any reasonable cause—there is no trouble, no sin, no warfare. I have learned that if my hands are clean and my heart is pure, it's time to press into intercession whether or not I ever know what I'm praying about—and I don't always know. I just answer the Holy Spirit's call.

When God Works through Emotions

That scene in Nicaragua was a memorable lesson for me, and it was later reinforced by the teachings of E. M. Bounds, a saint who lived from 1835 to 1913. He may or may not have known it, but he was prophetic. He was certainly a man of prayer. He said things like this:

> We have in the Holy Spirit an illustration and an enabler of what this intercession is and ought to be. We are charged to supplicate in the Spirit and to pray in the Holy Spirit. We are reminded that the Holy Spirit "helpeth our infirmities," and that while intercession is an art of so Divine and so high a nature that though we know not what to pray for as we ought, yet the Spirit teaches us this Heavenly science, by making intercession in us "with groanings which cannot be uttered." How burdened these intercessions of the Holy Spirit! How profoundly He feels the world's sin, the world's woe, and the world's loss, and how deeply He sympathizes with the dire conditions, are seen in His groanings which are too deep for utterance and too sacred to be voiced by Him. He inspires us to this most Divine work of intercession, and His strength enables us to sigh unto God for the oppressed, the burdened and the distressed creation. The Holy Spirit helps us in many ways.
>
> How intense will be the intercessions of the saints who supplicate in the spirit. How vain and delusive and how utterly fruitless and inefficient are prayers without the Spirit![8]

E. M. Bounds understood prayer burdens. He understood how to recognize them. Do you? Sometimes God places someone on your heart and you pray. That kind of prayer burden is not difficult to recognize. But many times a spiritual weight comes with a prayer burden like the one I felt in Nicaragua. I would describe it as:

- A heaviness of heart
- A restless mind
- A spirit of mourning
- Depressed emotions that seem to come on us out of nowhere

When this happens, we may think it's just our own emotions. So what do we do? We focus on ourselves rather than pressing into intercession. A wise prophetic friend once explained it this way: "When these feelings come to us, the flesh wants us to focus on me, me, me and turn it inward. The Spirit wants us to focus on them, them, them, and turn to intercession."

With that in mind, let's consider some scriptures that compare the flesh to the Spirit to drive this wisdom home:

- Jesus said to "watch and pray" and that "the spirit indeed is willing, but the flesh is weak" (Matt. 26:41).
- Jesus also said, "The Spirit gives life; the flesh counts for nothing" (John 6:63, NIV).
- The apostle Paul said, "Let the Holy Spirit guide your lives. Then you won't be doing what your sinful nature craves" (Gal. 5:16, NLT). What does your sinful nature crave? Self-gratification.
- Paul also said, "For they that are after the flesh do mind the things of the flesh; but they that are after the Spirit the things of the Spirit…So then

they that are in the flesh cannot please God. But ye are not in the flesh, but in the Spirit, if so be that the Spirit of God dwell in you" (Rom. 8:5, 8–9, KJV).

- A few chapters later, Paul said, "But put on the Lord Jesus Christ, and make no provision for the flesh to fulfill its lusts" (Rom. 13:14).
- Paul also said, "For the flesh lusts against the Spirit, and the Spirit against the flesh. These are in opposition to one another, so that you may not do the things that you please" (Gal. 5:17).
- And again Paul said, "For the one who sows to his own flesh will from the flesh reap corruption, but the one who sows to the Spirit will from the Spirit reap eternal life" (Gal. 6:8).

So what's my point?

When you feel heavy-hearted, when you feel depressed, when you feel oppressed, and when you feel out of sorts, don't get into your mind about it. Even if it is your own personal problem, getting into your mind is not going to solve it. Pray in the Spirit. He is willing to help you with your infirmities, and He wants to pray through you to help the infirmities of others.

Remember, the spirit is willing but the flesh is weak. Walk after the Spirit and you won't fulfill the lusts of the flesh. And get passionate about intercession. I'll leave you with another quote from E. M. Bounds:

> Desire burdens the chariot of prayer, and faith drives its wheels. Prayerless praying has no burden, because no sense of need; no ardency, because no vision, strength, or glow of faith. No mighty pressure to prayer, no holding on to God with the deathless, despairing grasp,

> "I will not let thee go except thou bless me." No utter self-abandon, lost in the throes of a desperate, pertinacious, and consuming plea: "Yet now if thou wilt forgive their sin—if not, blot me, I pray thee, out of thy book."[9]

What Is the Holy Spirit Trying to Tell You?

Although the Holy Spirit speaks expressly, we see through a glass darkly (1 Cor. 13:12). Sure, it's easy enough to understand the words of that still, small voice in your spirit. But impressions, dreams, and visions aren't always as clear as we'd like them to be—and reasoning blocks discernment.

I remember a time when a friend of mine was planning a trip to Los Angeles. She told me she was nervous about going, but I reasoned that it was a natural case of "the nerves" because she had an important meeting there. The week before she left, I started to get impressions that something bad was going to happen to her in Los Angeles. But it was like seeing through a glass darkly.

This was a call to intercession. I had no idea exactly what the enemy had planned, but you don't need to have all the details to stand in the gap. I pled the blood of Jesus and claimed the promises in Psalm 91 over my friend every day. The impressions—what I reasoned were fearful imaginations—didn't stop. Keep in mind I never had a clear word of the Lord come unto me. Again, this was a call to intercession.

For example, thoughts crossed my mind of a bad car accident. Thoughts crossed my mind of what I would do if she were killed in a car accident. I cast down those imaginations and every high and lofty thing that exalted itself against the knowledge of God and instead proclaimed the knowledge of God over her, continually pleading the blood of Jesus, rebuking every assignment of the enemy, and claiming protection over her life. I did this every day for the week before she left.

I never told my friend about this because, honestly, I was seeing through a glass darkly. I reasoned that it was just a spirit of fear coming against my mind in the midst of a trial. Reasoning blocks discernment. What I didn't know was that my friend was having dreams about a bad accident on her trip. She reasoned that it was just a spirit of fear coming against her mind. She never shared it with me. Reasoning blocks discernment.

My friend was hit head-on by a drunk driver at 8:30 a.m. while sitting in the back of a taxicab. The seat belts were broken. All she could do was brace for impact. At about 8:35 a.m. I received a text message from her phone with three characters: "911." When I called back, another voice on the line told me the terrible news and informed me my friend had a broken nose and fractured cheekbones and was being examined for other injuries. I felt horrible about what had happened. I felt somewhat responsible. But the Comforter quickly arrived on the scene to remind me that I had prayed over her every day and that prayer played a role in saving her life. I didn't know she was having the same impressions.

Did the warnings give my friend the presence of mind she needed to see the truck coming before it hit the taxi, crouch down between the seats, and brace herself for the impact? Did my prayers allow God to prevent more suffering and loss, and maybe even save her life? I believe so. Intercession doesn't always stop the enemy's assignment, but it can lessen the blow. Despite our reasoning and failure to communicate with one another about the warnings, the Holy Spirit got through enough to cause us both to take actions that minimized the damage.

So what's the lesson from all this? If you aren't sure something is the Holy Ghost, ask Him. When the Holy Ghost shows you something, press in to seek more details. When the Holy

Spirit gives you an impression, ask Him if you are supposed to share it with someone else or just pray. And always pray. The same God who is giving you the prophetic warning and unction for intercession will tell you what to do next if you ask Him. He will lead you and guide you into all truth that you need to know because He is the Spirit of truth.

Burden Bearing for the Lord

The principle of intercession includes burden bearing. Where I live they frequently plant new palm trees, and when they do, they use three stakes of wood to hold them steady until they are rooted and grounded in the soil. Those stakes bear the burden of the tree. When we intercede for people or places—whether we know what we are praying for or not—we stake ourselves to them and work with the Holy Spirit to remove what doesn't belong there. Dutch Sheets goes into this in detail in his book *Intercessory Prayer.*

Jesus is our model intercessor. First Peter 2:24 explains that He "bore our sins in His own body on the tree, that we, being dead to sins, should live unto righteousness. 'By His wounds you were healed.'" Jesus ever lives to make intercession for us (Heb. 7:25). At times, our intercession turns into all-out warfare. Again, we may not even know why. But we rely on the Holy Spirit to pray with and through us. As Paul wrote:

> Likewise, the Spirit helps us in our weaknesses, for we do not know what to pray for as we ought, but the Spirit Himself intercedes for us with groanings too deep for words. He who searches the hearts knows what the mind of the Spirit is, because He intercedes for the saints according to the will of God.
>
> —Romans 8:26–27

Sometimes we may know exactly what we are praying for but we don't know how to pray. The key to fruitful intercession—to effective burden bearing for the Lord—is to cooperate with the Holy Spirit. The Holy Spirit feels the same burden and is sharing with you so you can work with Him to bring His will to pass over people, situations, and even nations. Pray in the Spirit as much as you can, and you will develop greater discernment to recognize the burden of the Lord. And again, remember this:

> Intercessors, as we move deeper and deeper into the things of God, it's increasingly vital to learn to divide soul from spirit. When the burden of the Lord comes upon you, you may feel the weight of oppression, hear the enemy's accusations, or experience various negative emotions seemingly out of the blue. That's not you! Learn to quickly discern the call to pray against a thing rather than coming up under it.[10]

Amen.

Chapter 4

PRAYING IN THE SPIRIT

I'LL ADMIT IT: the first time I saw people praying in tongues, it completely freaked me out. It actually scared me!

The year was 1993. I was doing an internship at a Christian television station. Before going live on the air, the producers, cameramen, on-air talent, and others stood in a circle holding hands and praying in tongues just as fast and hard as they could. I looked on with confusion for a few minutes; then I left as fast as I could, thinking to myself, "Those people are crazy."

I was living with my grandparents at the time and told my grandfather what happened. He explained to me that this practice was of the devil. That sealed the deal for me. I never stepped foot back in that television studio. What's more, I mocked this supernatural experience. Of course, I wasn't born again and had no biblical knowledge of this spiritual practice.

I was flat-out ignorant, and it was my loss in the end. I didn't realize they were praying in the Spirit to build themselves up in their most holy faith (Jude 1:20). I didn't understand the level of warfare the prince of the power of the air wages against Christians in media. I didn't have any comprehension of prayer, much less praying in a heavenly language to compensate for our weakness.

Now I get it. Fast-forward twenty years, and now I pray in tongues for extended periods every day. I pray in tongues every chance I get. I pray in tongues in my car. I pray in tongues in the shower. I pray in tongues while I exercise. I pray in tongues while I clean my house. It's automatic now. If I'm not talking to someone or sleeping or writing, I'm most likely praying in tongues.

When it comes to spiritual warfare—and intercession—many times we don't know how to pray as we ought (Rom. 8:26). We sense spiritual oppression trying to discourage us, demons harassing people we love, or principalities settling over our city like a dark rain cloud—but we don't always have revelation about the enemy we are fighting.

When that happens, I always do one thing—pray in the Spirit. And I don't stop praying in the Spirit until that oppression lifts or until I have a Spirit-inspired strategy to wrestle against what's wrestling against me. I wrestle from a place of victory, but I don't wrestle presumptuously. I need the Holy Spirit to show me how to pray.

Building Yourself Up for War

Praying in the Spirit is a prerequisite to waging prophetic warfare. Think about it for a minute: before a soldier goes to war, he goes through grueling physical training to prepare himself for the battlefield. Take the US Army Basic Combat Training as an example. The training aims to transform a civilian into a soldier in ten weeks. The training prepares soldiers physically and mentally so they can withstand the physical strain of combat. Why should it be any different in the spirit?

We are in a war, and that means we will fight many battles before our ultimate victory. Before we head to the battlefield, we need to be physically, mentally, and spiritually prepared for what we might face so we can withstand the strain of spiritual combat. Remember, the battle is largely against our souls—our mind, will, and emotions—so we need to build ourselves up in our most holy faith to stand and withstand in the evil day. We need to build up our spirit man for war so our spirit man will lead and we will not be sidelined by our mind, will, and emotions.

Jude 17–20 says this:

> But, beloved, remember the words that were previously spoken by the apostles of our Lord Jesus Christ. They said to you, "In the last days there will be scoffers who will walk after their own ungodly desires." These are the men who cause divisions, sensual, devoid of the Spirit. But you, beloved, build yourselves up in your most holy faith. Pray in the Holy Spirit.

In chapter 2 we talked about carnal weapons versus mighty weapons. One way to guard ourselves against using carnal weapons—and one way to ensure we leverage our mighty weapons—is to pray in the Spirit. Praying in the Spirit builds us up in our most holy faith. I like the way the Amplified Bible, Classic Edition translates Jude 20: "But you, beloved, build yourselves up [founded] on your most holy faith [make progress, rise like an edifice higher and higher], praying in the Holy Spirit."

When we pray in the Spirit, we are accelerating our spiritual growth. If there is fear in our hearts, the Holy Spirit works to push out that fear so we become spiritual giants on the battlefield. David ran to the battle line with a prophetic strategy that took out his Goliath. We can expect to do the same when we pray in the Spirit.

When we pray in the Spirit, we are making spiritual progress against our enemies whether we can see it or not. Unbeknownst to us, the Holy Spirit is dealing with issues in our lives that open the door for the enemy. He is purging our hearts of fear, doubt, unbelief, selfishness, pride, and other hooks with which the enemy can snag us. When we pray in the Spirit, we are more likely to get God's perspective on the battlefield because like an edifice we are rising higher and higher in the Spirit.

Praying in the Spirit does much more than prepare us for war, but getting us ready to go toe to toe with principalities and powers in a supernatural wrestling match is certainly one of the benefits. Jude wasn't merely making a friendly suggestion when he said, "Pray in the Holy Spirit." He was offering a prophetic warfare strategy that will keep our spirits prepared for war and make us strong in the Lord and the power of His might so we won't back down from the good fight of faith.

Consider this. Before Paul told the church at Ephesus to put on their prophetic armor, he made this statement: "Finally, my brothers, be strong in the Lord and in the power of His might. Put on the whole armor of God that you may be able to stand against the schemes of the devil" (Eph. 6:10–11). Praying in the Spirit is the best way I know to prepare ourselves to wield our mighty weapons and fulfill Paul's marching orders outlined in the rest of Ephesians 6.

Do You Really Know How to Pray?

Do you really know how to pray? I'm sure you're an expert intercessor; but before you answer that question, consider Paul's warning not to think more highly of yourself than you ought (Rom. 12:3). We know that "knowledge puffs up" (1 Cor. 8:1, NKJV). With all due respect, no matter how seasoned you are, you still need the Holy Spirit's help to pray prophetically. But the good news is that even if you are new to intercession, the Holy Spirit can give you wisdom beyond your years.

I can say all that with confidence because, just as you probably have, I've read—and memorized—Romans 8:26–27. In case you need a reminder, it says this:

> Likewise, the Spirit helps us in our weaknesses, for we do not know what to pray for as we ought, but the Spirit Himself intercedes for us with groanings too deep for words. He who searches the hearts knows what the mind of the Spirit is, because He intercedes for the saints according to the will of God.

I'm quite sure Paul knew how to touch heaven with his prayers. Nevertheless, he would be the first to tell you that he didn't really know what to pray for sometimes. Sure, the need is sometimes evident. If someone is sick, they need prayers for healing. If someone has lost a loved one, they need the Comforter. If someone is oppressed by a devil, they need deliverance prayers. But many times we don't really know how to pray. And oftentimes we think we know what to pray for, and we are partly right, but there is much more to the story than meets the eye.

I agree with Paul's Spirit-inspired words. We don't know how to pray as we ought. Paul explains that the Spirit "helps" us. The Greek word for *help* in that verse is *sunantilambanomai*, which means "to lay hold along with, to strive to obtain with others, help in obtaining; to take hold with another."[1] That means the Holy Spirit is not doing the praying for us. He is doing the praying with us. He is helping us pray a perfect prayer—the perfect will of God.

Do you think the Holy Spirit would pray out of line with the Father's will? Of course not; but we might because of our weaknesses. The Greek word for *weakness* in this verse is *astheneia* and means "want of strength, weakness, infirmity."[2] We might ask with wrong motives to get what we want. We may ask for the wrong thing because we don't know what the right thing is. We might not have the boldness to ask for what we really need. We may be too scared to ask for what God really wants to do in and through us. Praying in the Spirit eliminates all those mays and mights, and prays out mysteries.

Paul explains: "For he who speaks in an unknown tongue does not speak to men, but to God. For no one understands him, although in the spirit, he speaks mysteries" (1 Cor. 14:2). What are those mysteries? They are often unknown, unless they manifest themselves in the natural. See, the devil can't understand what you are praying in tongues any more than you can. Sometimes God will reveal to you what you are praying for, but many times He will let it remain a mystery until the appointed time.

The Greek word for *mystery* in this verse is *musterion*, which means "hidden thing, secret, mystery...a hidden purpose or counsel, a secret will...the secret counsels which govern God in dealing with the righteous, which are hidden from ungodly and wicked men but plain to the godly," according to *The KJV New Testament Greek Lexicon*.[3] When I was a child, I read Encyclopedia Brown mysteries. But I've put aside childish things now and spend most of my free time worshipping, studying, praying—and especially praying out the mysteries of God in my life. That's scriptural.

Unlocking Warfare Strategies

In the context of spiritual warfare, Paul tells us in Ephesians 6:18: "Pray in the Spirit always with all kinds of prayer and supplication. To that end be alert with all perseverance and supplication for all the saints."

"When we don't know how to pray as we should, we can turn the intercession over to the Holy Spirit, and it will go directly to the heart of the matter with the wisdom and power of God to meet the need," says Bill Hamon, founder and bishop of Christian International Ministries Network, a coalition of over 3,700 ministers. "Using the spirit language, we can wage spiritual warfare against unseen enemies."[4]

There are many different kinds of prayer: supplication, petition, the prayer of faith that heals the sick. But praying in the Spirit gives us an edge in spiritual warfare—more so than all of these kinds of prayer—because we are praying out the mysteries of which Paul spoke.

It's interesting to me that the very first definition of *mystery* in *Merriam-Webster* does not relate to solving a murder or finding a criminal. In fact, the very first definition is "a religious truth that one can know only by revelation and cannot fully understand."[5]

The Bible speaks often of mysteries. For example, "great is the mystery of godliness" (1 Tim. 3:16). Paul speaks of the mystery of the restoration of Israel (Rom. 11:25–27) and the mystery of Jesus Christ (Rom. 16:25). The apostles spoke "the wisdom of God in a mystery, the hidden wisdom, which God ordained before the ages for our glory" (1 Cor. 2:7). Paul explained the mystery of the resurrection to the church at Corinth (1 Cor. 15:51). God has revealed at least one mystery to us: "to unite all things in Christ" (Eph. 1:9–10). The gospel is a mystery (Eph. 6:19). God is a mystery (Col. 2:2).

The type of mystery we can unlock in spiritual warfare through praying in tongues is the hidden wisdom Paul speaks of in 1 Corinthians 2:7. The word *wisdom* in this verse comes from the Greek word *sophia*, which pertains to spiritual wisdom.[6] If there is one thing we need in spiritual warfare, it is spiritual wisdom and revelation. When we pray in the Spirit, I believe it unlocks that spiritual wisdom and revelation, illuminating the enemy's plans in our spirits and offering us insight we need to launch a preemptive strike or take authority over a demonic assignment coming against our lives.

There is saying in Nicaragua, where I ministered each summer for about eight years, that "a devil exposed is a devil defeated." Praying in tongues can unlock hidden wisdom that reveals the enemy's plots and plans against us.

I still remember the day I stood with a group of prophetic intercessors praying on the land of our pastors, who were in the midst of a major home renovation. Everything that could go wrong was going wrong. A project that should have been done in six months had dragged out over a year. While we were praying in tongues, the Holy Spirit revealed a spirit of delay was operating. We took authority over that spirit, and wouldn't you know it, the project was wrapped up quickly.

At Awakening House of Prayer, my home base in Hollywood, Florida, I was praying in the Spirit during an altar call. My good friend Ryan LeStrange was calling out words of knowledge over various health issues. The Holy Spirit revealed to me that spiritual witchcraft was oppressing many in the room. I called for everyone battling witchcraft to stand up, and almost every single person rose for prayer.

Another time, one of my intercessors was praying in diverse tongues over a troubling situation and suddenly began to cry out the interpretation, "Shut the mouth of the enemy!" With that revelation, she bound the accuser of the brethren, and peace came almost immediately between two leaders in the body of Christ who were at odds with one another.

When we pray in tongues, sometimes the Holy Spirit comes alongside us to root out, pull down, destroy, and throw down. I believe He is getting rid of the hooks in our flesh that the enemy can use to trip us up and moving obstacles that we don't even know exist so we don't stumble along the path to our destiny. Again, sometimes we get the revelation of what we are praying, but sometimes we may never know.

"When in the heat of spiritual combat, it is easy to start praying prayers that agree with the size of the attack, emphasizing the problem rather than focusing on the size of the blood-bought victory that Jesus purchased at the cross," says Larry Sparks, author of *Breakthrough Faith* and host of the weekly radio program *Voice of Destiny*.[7]

"Praying in tongues empowers you to agree with God's victorious battle plan for your life and your circumstances, no matter what is going on around you. It does not deny reality; it simply positions you to agree with the higher truth of Scripture: Victory has been purchased, and it is yours through Jesus Christ."[8]

I believe praying in tongues builds me up (1 Cor. 14:4, 18) as I speak directly to God (1 Cor. 14:2, 14). I believe praying in tongues stirs my faith (Jude 20). I believe praying in tongues assures that I am praying God's perfect will (Rom. 8:26–27). I believe there are many benefits to praying in tongues. That's why I do it as much as I can, and I encourage other believers to do the same.

Staying on the Offense

By praying in tongues, we can stay on the offense against the enemy. We know that the devil roams about like a roaring lion seeking someone to devour (1 Pet. 5:8). We know that the enemy comes to steal, kill, and destroy (John 10:10). Praying in the Spirit is one way that we can fulfill the scriptural exhortation to "pray without ceasing" (1 Thess. 5:17).

Praying in tongues also builds the fruit of the Spirit in our spirits. When we pray in the Spirit, we walk in the Spirit. In Galatians 5:16–26, Paul offered this wisdom from heaven:

> I say then, walk in the Spirit, and you shall not fulfill the lust of the flesh. For the flesh lusts against the Spirit,

> and the Spirit against the flesh. These are in opposition to one another, so that you may not do the things that you please. But if you are led by the Spirit, you are not under the law.
>
> Now the works of the flesh are revealed, which are these: adultery, sexual immorality, impurity, lewdness, idolatry, sorcery, hatred, strife, jealousy, rage, selfishness, dissensions, heresies, envy, murders, drunkenness, carousing, and the like. I warn you, as I previously warned you, that those who do such things shall not inherit the kingdom of God.
>
> But the fruit of the Spirit is love, joy, peace, patience, gentleness, goodness, faith, meekness, and self-control; against such there is no law. Those who are Christ's have crucified the flesh with its passions and lusts. If we live in the Spirit, let us also walk in the Spirit. Let us not be conceited, provoking one another and envying one another.

I am convinced through practical experience that the more we pray in the Spirit, the less we will look for something to satisfy the lust of the flesh. The lust of the flesh is a major inroad for the enemy in our lives, and we need all the help we can get to crucify our flesh. I am convinced through practical experience that praying in the Spirit helps us to avoid the temptation to tap into the works of the flesh, which—if you believe Paul's Spirit-inspired words—clearly has severe consequences. Finally, I am convinced through practical experience that praying in the Spirit helps mature the fruit of the Spirit in our lives. The fruit of the Spirit is part of our mighty weapons.

When we walk in love with those who are not lovely, we are moving in the opposite spirit of the enemy. That is spiritual warfare. When we bless those who curse us, we are demonstrating the love of God. That is spiritual warfare. When we walk in peace in chaotic situations, we are showing the devil we trust God. Paul told the church at Philippi: "Do not be frightened by your adversaries. This is a sign to them of their destruction, but of your salvation, and this from God" (Phil. 1:28). We also know that the peace of God, which surpasses understanding, is an offensive weapon because it protects our hearts and minds through Christ Jesus (Phil. 4:7).

The fruit of patience is a spiritual warfare weapon. In 1990, a *New York Times* columnist suggested patience was America's best weapon in the Gulf War.[9] Patience can keep us from speaking out the enemy's plan over our lives and giving him the power to execute it by our agreement. Waiting on the Lord to vindicate us instead of taking matters into our own hands requires patience. Love itself is patient.

We know that Christ is gentle, but He is also a warrior. "A soft answer turns away wrath, but a harsh word stirs up anger" (Prov. 15:1, ESV); God's wisdom is gentle (James 3:17). Goodness is a spiritual weapon because when we do good, we move in direct opposition to our spiritual enemies, which are evil. Doing good when bad things are happening to you—giving your enemy a drink of water—is spiritual warfare. Of course, faith, humility, and self-control are also applicable in warfare and are weapons.

Puffed Up Spiritual Warriors

Did you know it's possible to flow in pride in our spiritual warfare skills, which can cause God to resist us even while we are trying to resist the devil? Indeed, we can actually take pride in our spiritual warfare skills—and many do. I came out of a spiritual warfare camp some years ago that was especially proud of its brute battle force. We considered ourselves the Navy Seals of spiritual warfare. Yet the devil rarely fled. It seemed as if there was never any lasting breakthrough. Even David has seasons of rest from war (2 Sam. 7:1).

Pride in our spiritual warfare skills can cause us to stumble before our enemies because "God resists the proud, but gives grace to the humble" (1 Pet. 5:5). We need the grace of God to overcome our enemies. Flaunting our spiritual warfare skills like a boastful five-star general will most certainly lead to some measure of defeat at some point.

But it's not just pride in our warfare skills that can hinder our effectiveness in destroying strongholds. It's pride in any area of our life. Of course, we all have a measure of pride in our carnal nature. But when the Holy Spirit is dealing with us about pride in some area—or when we see our own pride—and we don't cry out for the grace of humility, we are walking in sheer disobedience. The Bible says we are to have a "readiness to revenge all disobedience, when your obedience is fulfilled" (2 Cor. 10:6, KJV). I believe the more we seek to walk in obedience to the Word of God, the more effective we will be in spiritual warfare.

In our flesh, we are no match for the devil. We need the power of the Holy Spirit to back up our authority in Christ to root out, pull down, destroy, throw down, build, and plant. We can't drive demons into obedience to the Word of God when we are blatantly disobeying the Word of God in any area, whether it's walking in pride or some other sin.

And that brings me back to one of the key points in this chapter: Praying in the Spirit will help us crucify our flesh. It helps us posture our hearts to die to self, be more sensitive to the Spirit's conviction, and be quick to repent.

Chapter 5

PROPHETIC DREAMS THAT UNLOCK SPIRITUAL WARFARE STRATEGIES

A SPIDER WAS SPINNING a web in the corner. The web was rapidly growing larger before my eyes, almost like a time lapse video that reveals the progression of a blooming flower. I watched, almost paralyzed with fear, and then decided to go look for some reinforcement from spiritual warriors far more experienced than I was at that time.

A spiderweb serves as a net to capture prey. I knew the enemy was weaving a wicked web of deception. I didn't know who the target was. I just knew the spider was humongous and its web even larger. This spider was trying to take over! I found one of my spiritual mentors and brought her to the scene. She looked on, unmoved.

"Well, do something," I implored.

"You don't need me to take authority over this assignment. You bind it in the name of Jesus and it will flee," she replied.

At that moment, righteous indignation and holy boldness rose up in my spirit and I began to take authority over principalities and powers in the name of Jesus. I started binding the spirit of witchcraft. I pled the blood of Jesus against it. I declared it was under my feet and canceled the assignment. Of course, you know what happened. The spiderweb was dismantled.

Then I woke up. It sounds simple, but the Holy Spirit was revealing to me in a prophetic dream that I needed to stop depending on others to do my spiritual warfare. As a young believer, I needed to rise up in the authority He gave me in His Son and command the devil to bow to the name above all names. Sometimes the only way God can get through to us is in our dreams.

The Lord had to show me pictures of myself taking authority over this enemy attack in my dreams to make it clear that it was time for me to come up higher—that I was well able to get the victory over a spirit that had been bringing weariness, infirmities, and oppression in my life. The strategy in itself was not profound, but seeing myself gaining the victory in the dream gave me more confidence that God was with me, because He showed me He was. In more recent years, I wrote a book about it titled *Satan's Deadly Trio: Defeating the Deceptions of Jezebel, Religion and Witchcraft*. If you are battling witchcraft, that is a great title to pick up.

Dreaming Prophetic Dreams

Not everybody is a dreamer in the sense that they have heavy prophetic dreams revealing events to come—or prophetic warfare strategies that turn situations in their favor. But I do believe every believer has the capacity to dream prophetically. Even unbelievers like Pharaoh in Joseph's day and King Nebuchadnezzar in Daniel's day had prophetic dreams. Of course, they couldn't interpret them because the interpretations belong to God (Gen. 40:8).

Spirit-filled Christians love to quote Joel 2:28 in the context of dreams in the last days, so I'll share it with you again (even though you probably already have it memorized) to make the point: "And it will be that, afterwards, I will pour out My Spirit on all flesh; then your sons and your daughters will prophesy, your old men will dream dreams, and your young men will see visions."

Peter recited those verses after Pentecost and declared we are in those days (Acts 2:17). An increase in dream activity is related to an outpouring of the Spirit. What do the Greek and Hebrew words for *dream* mean in these scriptures? Quite simply, "dream." *Merriam-Webster* defines *dream* as "a series of thoughts, visions, or feelings that happen during sleep."[1]

The word *dreams* in Joel 2:28 and Acts 2:17 makes the meaning more explicit. The Hebrew word *chalowm* can mean an ordinary dream, but in this context I believe it refers to its second definition, which is a dream "with prophetic meaning."[2] That is because the Greek word for *dream* in the corresponding Acts 2:17 is *enupniazomai*, which means "to dream (divinely suggested) dreams."[3]

David understood that God spoke to him in dreams when he wrote, "I will bless the LORD who has given me counsel; my affections also instruct me in the night seasons" (Ps. 16:7). And Job 33:14–18 demonstrates divinely suggested dreams:

> For God speaks once, yes twice, yet man does not perceive it. In a dream, in a vision of the night, when deep sleep falls upon men, in slumber on their beds, then He opens the ears of men, and seals their instruction, that He might turn aside man from his purpose, and conceal pride from man. He keeps back his soul from the pit, and his life from perishing by the sword.

In the Old Testament and New, God used dreams to communicate with His people. Consider Jacob's dream of the ladder set up on the earth with the top of it reaching to the heaven, and angels of God ascending and descending on it (Gen. 28:12). Laban was warned in a dream not to speak good or bad to Jacob (Gen. 31:24). We all know about Joseph's dream, which landed him in a pit and a prison before God promoted him to the palace to save countless lives during a famine (Gen.

37:9–11). God spoke to Solomon, Pharaoh, the Midianites, Pilate's wife, Joseph, Gideon, Pharaoh's chief butler and baker, the three wise men, and many others through dreams.

Prophetic dreams bring revelation, including spiritual warfare strategies. When it comes to prophetic warfare dreams, I believe the gift of discerning of spirits is operating within the dreams. Mentioned immediately after the gift of prophecy in 1 Corinthians 12:10, the gift of discerning of spirits is a supernatural ability to judge between what is true and false; it is a spiritual facility to discern the presence of the Holy Spirit or the presence of an evil spirit operating.

All Christians have some measure of discernment, but the gift of discerning of spirits goes beyond good discernment into the supernatural reality—and this can operate in dreams just the same as it operates when we are awake. Of course, the first thing you should do in response to any prophetic dream that suggests warfare is pray.

You pray for the interpretation if it is not evident—and even if it is evident, because there are often layers—and you pray out the strategy the Holy Spirit gives you in the dream. If you did not get a clear strategy in the dream, then pray some more. The Holy Spirit who gave you the dream is the same Holy Spirit who knows the strategy to overcome the opposition, whether that is performing some prophetic act, fasting, engaging in deep intercession, or even making some natural move.

Warning Dreams

When I first entered into prophetic ministry, I received warnings, warnings, and more warnings from the Lord about what the enemy was doing or wanted to do. It seemed like almost every prophetic word I had was a warning, and no one really wanted to hear it. Most people prefer the bless-me-only prophets. I believe in prophesying blessings when God is speaking blessings, but I also believe in prophesying the warning when God is offering a warning. Don't you?

In one warning dream, I was in a church—back at the sound booth—when two men wearing black cowboy hats and dressed in dark clothes entered the sanctuary. Nobody seemed to notice them. They were armed and dangerous, yet no one stopped them. They proceeded to walk through the sanctuary and back toward the kids' church area. I watched this unfold and felt grave danger was imminent.

The meaning of the warning was this: a murderous religious spirit was working to infiltrate the church and would move through the sanctuary and even infect the kids. The prophetic warfare strategy was obvious: coming against the spirit of religion in intercession. Of course, in the natural we were also on alert for the workings of the religious spirit operating in our midst. We relied on discernment to root out religious thinking even in our own souls that would hinder God's work.

God's heart with warning dreams is to give you a heads up so you can engage in spiritual warfare to break the assignment in the spirit realm before it hits the natural realm. The prophetic warfare strategy, then, is contained within the dream in the sense that our response is always to break, bind, take authority over, and otherwise come against the impending danger, whether it is a spirit, a storm, an economic crisis, or some other manner of trial. Consider the warning King Abimelek received in a dream in Genesis 20:3–7:

> But God came to Abimelek in a dream by night and said to him, "You are a dead man because of the woman whom you have taken, for she is a man's wife."
>
> Abimelek had not gone near her, and he said, "Lord, will You slay a righteous nation? Did he not say to me, 'She is my sister,' and did not even she herself say, 'He is

> my brother'? In the integrity of my heart and innocence of my hands I have done this."
>
> And God said to him in a dream, "Yes, I know that you did this in the integrity of your heart. For I also kept you from sinning against Me. Therefore, I did not let you touch her. Therefore return the man's wife, for he is a prophet and he will pray for you. Moreover, you will live. However, if you do not return her, know that you will surely die, you and all who are yours."

Of course, every prophetic warning can't be prayed away. We can't pray away end-times prophecies. These things must be so. At times, the Holy Spirit shows us things to come in dreams so that we can prepare our hearts—and sometimes make natural preparations—for what lies ahead. Sometimes the prophetic warfare strategy, then, is not to stop what is coming but to overcome the battle in our minds that will result from the trial so we hold fast to our faith. God does not want us to be blindsided by the enemy, and He wants us to see the other side, not just the trial. Always look for the blessing in the storm.

Warning dreams are often misinterpreted, so I would urge you to take caution in applying a meaning. Again, the Holy Spirit who gave you the prophetic dream is the same Holy Spirit who will give you its meaning. Yes, He may use another person to give you the full meaning; but don't rely too much on people. Rely on God. Joseph interpreted two dreams God gave Pharaoh by the Spirit of God. You can read the entire account in Genesis 41, but the essence is this:

> The dreams of Pharaoh are one and the same. God has shown Pharaoh what He is about to do. The seven good cows are seven years, and the seven good ears are seven years. The dreams are one. The seven gaunt and

> ugly cows that came up after them are seven years, and the seven empty ears scorched by the east wind will be seven years of famine.
>
> —Genesis 41:25–27

Thanks to Joseph's interpretation, Pharaoh had a strategy that saved many lives and ultimately gave him great authority and riches in the known world.

I have seen too many people buffeting the air, picking fights with dormant devils, because they missed the interpretation of a dream. Some people even attribute true dreams from God to the devil. Others simply ignore prophetic dreams of warning. Rick Joyner is not one of them. The founder of MorningStar Ministries shared with the body of Christ a disturbing dream he had about ISIS coming to America as the "Gate of Hell" has opened. "I have done in-depth studies of the cruelty in the Middle Ages, but this was a whole new level of demonic cruelty. It wasn't just about killing people," Joyner said. "It was about bringing as much absolute pain, terror and everything else you can before death."[4]

The bottom line: warning dreams aim to give us time to change our course of action, and that usually requires a combination of prayer and Spirit-inspired action. Intercession is vital even when it looks like judgment cannot be averted. "Mercy triumphs over judgment" (James 2:13).

Prophetic Dreams That Offer Warfare Revelation

Gideon was an unassuming fellow. He came on the Bible scene at a time when the Lord had given Israel into the hands of Midian for seven years. Whenever Israel would plant crops, Israel's enemies would ruin them. When Israel started crying out to the Lord for help, the Lord sent them a prophet who made it all too clear why they were in that situation: "I said to you, 'I am the Lord your God. Do not worship the gods of the Amorites in whose land you are living.' But you have disobeyed Me" (Judg. 6:10). But God nevertheless had a plan to deliver Israel. Again, mercy triumphs over judgment.

An angel of the Lord came to Gideon, who was threshing wheat in the wilderness to hide it from the Midianites. When the angel called him a "mighty man of valor," Gideon had just one question. Well, actually two: "If the Lord is with us, then why has all this happened to us? Where are all His miracles that our fathers told us about?" (Judg. 6:12–13). The angel did not answer Gideon, but rather asked him a question in response: "Go in this strength of yours. Save Israel from the control of Midian. Have I not sent you?" (Judg. 6:14).

Like Moses, Gideon could not see how he could possibly save Israel. He started confessing how weak he was and how young he was. But the angel assured him that he would overcome the enemies if he would fight. Gideon, still struggling with unbelief, boldly asked: "If I have found favor in Your sight, give me a sign that it is You who are speaking with me" (Judg. 6:15–17). He would get more than one in the end.

The immediate sign was fire rising out of a rock to consume meat and unleavened bread Gideon presented to the angel. Gideon thought He would die (Judg. 6:21–22). Of course, he didn't. Fast-forward a little while and you see Gideon with his army. Apparently he had assembled quite a team of men who were set to go against the Midianites, at least by outward appearance. But the Lord sees the heart.

Listen in to the scene in Judges 7:2–7:

> The Lord said to Gideon, "You have too many people with you for Me to give the Midianites into their hands, lest Israel glorify themselves over Me, saying, 'Our own power saved us.' So now, call out so the people can hear, 'Whoever is afraid or anxious may turn back and leave

> Mount Gilead.'" So twenty-two thousand from among the people turned back, and ten thousand were left.
>
> But the LORD said to Gideon, "There are still too many people. Bring them down to the water, and I will test them for you there. When I say to you, 'This one will go with you,' he will go with you. Everyone about whom I will say, 'This one will not go with you,' will not go."
>
> So he brought the people down to the water, and the LORD said to Gideon, "You shall set apart by himself everyone who laps the water with his tongue like dogs; likewise, everyone who kneels down to drink." The number of those who lapped, putting their hands to their mouths, was three hundred. The rest of the people had knelt to drink water.
>
> The LORD said to Gideon, "With three hundred men who lapped to drink, I will save you and give the Midianites into your hands. All the rest of the people should go home."

Even after all this, Gideon still wasn't confident. Maybe he was kin to doubting Thomas. That same night, Jehovah God told Gideon to get up and go down into the camp, and assured him the victory. Clearly Gideon was still afraid. The Lord sensed that and told him to go down into the camp with his servant Purah and listen to the conversation taking place. He promised Gideon he would be emboldened by this act of obedience (Judg. 7:9–11). Here is where the prophetic warfare strategy comes in. Let's read Judges 7:12–18:

> Now the Midianites, Amalekites, and the Kedemites covered the valley like locusts; and their camels could not be counted, for they were as numerous as grains of sand on the seashore.

> Gideon came and overheard one man who was telling his dream to another. The man said, "Listen to a dream I had. I saw a dry cake of barley bread rolling into the Midianite camp. It rolled up to a tent and struck it. It fell, turned upside down, and collapsed."
>
> The other man responded, "This is none other than the sword of Gideon son of Joash the Israelite. God has given Midian and the whole camp into his hands."
>
> When Gideon heard the telling of the dream and its interpretation, he worshipped, returned to the camp of Israel, and said, "Get up, for the LORD has given the Midianite camp into your hands." He divided the three hundred men into three combat units. He gave all of them ram's horn trumpets, empty jars, and torches within the jars.
>
> He said to them, "Look at me and do likewise. Watch, and when I come to the perimeter of the camp, do as I do. When I and all who are with me blow the horn, then you will blow the horns all around the camp and shout, "For the LORD and for Gideon!'"

Here is the end of the story: Gideon and one hundred men went to the edge of the Midianites' camp, where they blew horns and smashed jars, and held torches and cried out, "A sword for the LORD and for Gideon!" (Judg. 7:20). The men in the camp fled. When Gideon's three hundred men blew their horns in unison, the Lord brought confusion into the enemy's camp and they turned on each other (Judg. 7:22). Gideon's army won by executing this prophetic warfare strategy. You can be sure when the Holy Spirit gives you a prophetic warfare strategy in a dream, it will work just the same for you.

Principles for Dream Interpretation

Of course, we know that all dreams are not from God. I have heard some pretty goofy stuff over the years, and I am sure you have also. Sometimes it's just a pizza dream. In other words, you ate something too heavy or too spicy and it caused strange dreams. Other times, it's your subconscious working through an issue in the natural. Still other times, it's the enemy trying to work through your dream life to lead you astray or attack you in the night.

The preacher said, "For when there is an abundance of dreams and futilities, then words increase too. Therefore it is God you should fear" (Eccles. 5:7). You don't need to give voice to every dream you have. You need to pray and ask God if the dream is from Him, and be certain it is, or go to an elder who can help you judge it before you try to interpret it. You can sure waste a lot of time with foolish vanities if you aren't careful. I am convinced that God tries to speak to us more than we know, but sometimes we get too caught up with superfluous dreams and visions that aren't from Him to pay attention to what He is really saying.

Before we get into this topic of interpreting dreams, though, I want to caution you not to pick up a secular dream interpretation book or buy into the meaning of numbers, symbols, colors, animals, and other dream features that are outlined all over the Internet. Although there are certainly some legitimate sites that offer true biblical interpretations, you have to be extremely cautious because most of what you find is pure New Age divination—or worse, witchcraft.

There have been many, many books written on the topic of Christian dream interpretation. I won't seek to rehash every principle here, but I will go through some. There are many principles involved in interpreting dreams. One of them is numbers. In Pharaoh's dream, he saw seven lean cows and seven good cows, as well as seven good ears of corn and seven bad ears of corn (Gen. 41:17–32). This spoke to the seven-year cycle. There would be seven years of abundance and seven years of famine. Numbers can have meanings in dreams, but you still need the Holy Spirit's confirmation. Presumption can get you into trouble.

It is the same, of course, with symbols. Some symbols are easy to discern. Snakes, serpents, rats, and frogs clearly represent demons. You see it all through Scripture. A house can point to the state of your life or even your spiritual life. (See Matthew 7:24–27; 2 Timothy 2:20–21.) If your house is leaking, for example, that can speak of the need for more spiritual covering or even the need to repent. If you dream about rushing water, it signals the presence of the Holy Spirit. (See Ezekiel 47:1–9.)

There are many symbols that are not so easy to interpret, especially in the Book of Revelation. Likewise, you may dream dreams that are not so easy to interpret, but if a dream is from God, the meaning will come out sooner or later. You will recognize when the events start to unfold—even if you don't get the full meaning beforehand—and you can then respond appropriately. Sometimes dreams with symbols serve as a confirmation rather than a warning or a prophetic strategy.

Patterns are also important to discern. I have had a series of baby dreams over the years, though not in the perfect timeline order. I have dreamed I was pregnant and unhappy about it. I have dreamed I was about to deliver but couldn't get into the delivery room. I have dreamed that the baby seemed to be lifeless within me. I have dreamed of giving birth to a man-child, complete with a full head of hair, who started running as soon as he was born. None of these dreams came in sequence, and each had particular meaning. Some of the meaning was immediately apparent. Some has yet to be revealed.

Colors can have significance in dreams. Blue is known as a heavenly color. Red, the color of Jesus's blood, speaks to redemption, while purple signifies royalty. White, of course, symbolizes righteousness. You can see a lot of these meanings clearly in Scripture.

Animals in dreams can also have a number of meanings. I already told you about snakes, serpents, and frogs, but lambs represent Jesus. Rats and owls are unclean spirits, sheep relate to believers, and the Holy Spirit is represented as a dove.

The dream world can be complex, and you can't rely on a textbook alone. Guidelines like these can be tremendously helpful, but they can also limit your mind and shut out your understanding of what the Holy Spirit is really trying to show you. It takes Bible knowledge, spiritual sensitivity, and experience to rightly interpret dreams. Ultimately the revelation comes from God Himself. Flesh and blood cannot reveal the meanings of your dreams or your visions. In the next chapter, we will talk about seeing warfare tactics in prophetic visions.

Chapter 6

SEEING WARFARE TACTICS IN PROPHETIC VISIONS

The very first time our group of intercessors started praying out the prophetic words people prophesied over the State of Florida—a prophetic warfare strategy we will explore in greater detail in chapter 9—I had a vision of an arrow being put into a quiver (a case for carrying arrows).

The Holy Spirit showed me that these 1 Timothy 1:18 prayer calls were like arrows in our spiritual warfare quiver. In other words, the prayer call is a new weapon for a new season in which we find ourselves. This arrow in the quiver is a prophetic strategy that can be used to hit our prayer target. Our prayer target is awakening. We want to see Florida, widely known in prophetic circles as the Forerunner State or the First Fruits State, fulfill its destiny.

Since that day, we have launched these 1 Timothy 1:18 prayer calls in other states across the nation. There is, as we say, a lot of wind on this tactic. In other words, the Holy Spirit is really breathing on this prophetic warfare strategy in this season. There is an anointing to declare prophecies that have been released over our states—and our nation—in years and even decades past.

On these calls we invariably see a release of additional prophetic insight that launches us into deep intercession over our states. The Holy Spirit often releases instruction on how to pray in the next season. He co-labors with us as we tap into the prophetic vein and shows us things to come.

It is always powerful, and Paul the apostle knew this. That is why he told his spiritual son Timothy to "fight a good fight" according to the "prophecies that were previously given to you" (1 Tim. 1:18). The Amplified Bible, Classic Edition interprets this scripture, "This charge and admonition I commit in trust to you, Timothy, my son, in accordance with prophetic intimations which I formerly received concerning you, so that inspired and aided by them you may wage the good warfare."

Dreams come by night, but visions come by day. Especially during prophetic intercession, God can give you pictures or visions of warfare strategies and tactical battle plans. Think about it for a minute. The entire Book of Revelation is a prophetic vision that reveals God's end-times battle plans. In this chapter, we will explore God's prophetic visions to give His people instructions to push back darkness.

Ezekiel's Vision of Resurrection Power

Ezekiel had plenty of strange visions and walked out many odd prophetic acts. In one of his prophetic warfare visions, he saw the resurrection power of God. You will find the account in Ezekiel 37. Ezekiel leaves record of God's hand being on him, carrying him out in the spirit and setting him down in the midst of a valley of dry bones. Ezekiel assessed the situation for a few minutes until the Lord interrupted him with a question: "Son of man, can these bones live?" (Ezek. 37:3).

Ezekiel certainly didn't know the answer. From a natural perspective, it looked impossible. After all, the bones weren't just dry; they were very dry. And there weren't just a few bones in the valley; the bones were all around him. In other words, the presence of death and decay surrounded him. I imagine it was an overwhelming sight. The Lord did not let him linger there too long, but in the midst of this prophetic vision He gave him an apostolic instruction:

> Again He said to me, "Prophesy over these bones and say to them, O dry bones, hear the word of the LORD. Thus says the Lord GOD to these bones: I will cause breath to enter you so that you live. And I will lay sinews upon you and will grow back flesh upon you and cover you with skin and put breath in you so that you live. Then you shall know that I am the LORD."
>
> —EZEKIEL 37:4–6

In this passage—in the account of this vision—we see the Lord sharing a prophetic warfare strategy with Ezekiel. Despite the doom and gloom around him, Ezekiel obeyed the Lord's command and prophesied. I imagine he was surprised when there was a noise and a shaking even while the very words were coming out of his mouth. "The bones came together, bone to its bone" (Ezek. 37:7).

As he looked on, the sinews and the flesh grew upon them and skin covered them. But the job wasn't quite done—the resurrection was not complete. Ezekiel was still contending in the valley of dry bones. As he marveled over the manifestation of supernatural power, the Lord gave him another instruction: "Prophesy to the wind; prophesy, son of man, and say to the wind: Thus says the Lord GOD: Come from the four winds, O breath, and breathe upon these slain so that they live" (Ezek. 37:9).

With boldness Ezekiel prophesied the word of the Lord, and to his awe breath came into the bones. Those once-dry bones were resurrected to fullness of life. Ezekiel reported that they lived and stood up on their feet. What was once pile after pile of very dry bones in a vast valley was transformed into "an exceeding great army" (Ezek. 37:10). It is worth noting that only after Ezekiel was fully obedient was the mystery of his prophetic vision fully revealed to him.

> Then He said to me, "Son of man, these bones are the whole house of Israel. They say, 'Our bones are dried up, and our hope is lost. We are cut off completely.' Therefore prophesy and say to them, Thus says the Lord God: Pay attention, O My people, I will open your graves and cause you to come up out of your graves and bring you into the land of Israel. Then you shall know that I am the Lord, when I have opened your graves, O My people, and brought you up out of your graves. And I shall put My Spirit in you, and you shall live, and I shall place you in your own land. Then you shall know that I the Lord have spoken and performed it, says the Lord."
>
> —Ezekiel 37:11–14

Judah and Jerusalem were on the verge of destruction for sinning against Jehovah. There was little hope to be had. Israel was in a dead spiritual state; the bones were not only very dry but also scattered in a valley. In this prophetic vision, the Lord gave Ezekiel the strategy to deliver Israel from bondage. God showed Ezekiel how to pray over the nation so they could see His glory once again. Ezekiel looked past the discouraging state of the nation and into the grace of God and saw the deliverance of Israel. He prophesied with passion. He prayed with purpose. He warred with willingness to appear as a fool. And he saw a nation resurrected from the dead.

William Branham's Historic Vision

There is at least one recording in modern history of someone seeing a vision of resurrection and then witnessing the actual resurrection. William Branham, a prophet from southern Kentucky who rose to fame during the Voice of Healing movement and was known for healing manifestations with the help of an angel, had a vision in Georgia. (Although Branham ended his life in deception, thinking he was the prophet Elijah, he was for many years a very accurate prophet who saw much fruit in his ministry.)

"I seen a little boy being raised from the dead," Branham said. "I went down in Miami and there predicted it before thousands of people." Branham not only predicted it—he described to a tee what the young boy would look like, right down to his hairstyle and his eye color.[1]

Two years later, Branham was in Finland. After coming off the mountains one day, he went up into a watchtower. On his way down the road, he saw an American-made car strike two children. Branham said the car knocked one of the children into a tree and crushed his brains against a tree and the car's fender. The car had rolled over the other child and he was lying dead with some coats over him. As Branham tells it, his companions went over to look at the little boy and came back to him crying. They encouraged Branham to go see him, but he declined because he had a son nearly the same age.

"Finally, they persuaded me to go over and when I went to look at the little lad, I looked down at him and my heart was breaking to see the little fella, and I turned away," Branham said. "And when I turned away, something laid its hand on my shoulder. I thought it was brother Lindsay, and I looked around and there was nobody around me at all and the hand was still on my shoulder."[2]

According to Branham's account, the parents were on their way to the scene. The little boy had been dead about thirty minutes. Branham said he looked down twice and then asked someone to raise the coat off the little dead boy. At that moment, the Lord showed him the vision he had seen in

Georgia of a little boy being raised from the dead. It was the same boy lying on the ground!

"Every bone in his body was broken and his foot run through his sock. It was that boy perfectly...Oh my, what a feeling...You could take every scientist in the world and stand them there and every demon out of torment could be standing there—it's going to happen anyhow...God's already said it, and it's going to be done," Branham said. "I said if that little boy isn't on his feet in the next five minutes I'm a false prophet."[3]

As the story goes, Branham knelt down over the boy just as he had seen himself do in the vision, and prayed, "Lord, God of heavens and earth over in the homeland you showed me this vision while passing through Georgia one night...I pray to thee Lord God that now that you will confirm the word so they might know that you're still the Lord Jesus and that Finland might know that You are the resurrection from the dead."[4]

Branham laid his hands on the dead boy and called for death to give the boy back. Immediately, he said, the little boy jumped up screaming and running around. He was raised from the dead and his broken bones healed—all in an instant. The news spread all over Finland. The mayor certified the event, and it goes down in church history as one of the most astounding miracles ever. Branham waged prophetic warfare against death based on a vision from the Lord, and God was glorified.[5]

Is it possible that Jesus had prophetic visions of raising people from the dead? Did He see Himself raising Jairus's daughter from her deathbed? (See Luke 8:40–55.) Did He see Himself raising the Nain widow's son from the dead? (See Luke 7:11–15.) Did He see Himself raising Lazarus from the dead? (See John 11:1–44.) Why am I asking these questions? Because of what Jesus said:

> Then Jesus said to them, "Truly, truly I say to you, the Son can do nothing of Himself, but what He sees the Father do. For whatever He does, likewise the Son does. For the Father loves the Son and shows Him all things that He Himself does. And He will show Him greater works than these so that you may marvel. For as the Father raises the dead and gives them life, even so the Son gives life to whom He will."
>
> —John 5:19–21

Clearly, if Jesus only did what He saw the Father do, then He saw the resurrection in the spirit before He commanded the dead to be raised in the natural. The Father knew before Jairus's daughter, the widow's son, and Lazarus died that they would die—and He also knew they would be resurrected from the dead. The Father showed Jesus His will in the matter, and Jesus prayed and obeyed, waging prophetic warfare against the spirit of death. Of course, not all prophetic warfare visions deal with raising people from the dead—remember, the Book of Revelation is full of prophetic visions of warfare—but they will all breathe God's breath of life over a situation.

Open Our Eyes, Lord!

It has been said that we don't know what we don't know, but it is just as true that we can't see what we can't see. Sometimes the enemy has so clouded our vision that we need God to break in with light—to open our eyes wide so we can see the supernatural events unfolding behind the natural scenes.

I've been there. Although we walk by faith instead of by sight (2 Cor. 5:7), sometimes God will choose to let us see something supernatural to bolster our faith—or just to get our attention when we are going astray.

When God opens our eyes, it may be in the form of a prophetic dream, a vision, a trance, or even what feels like a real-life experience in heaven or hell. Although we should not seek supernatural experiences for the sake of seeking supernatural experiences, we should seek God and trust that He will give us what we need. There is nothing wrong with crying out to God to open your eyes when you sense that you aren't seeing what He really wants you to see. Like I said, I've been there—and so have Balaam and Elisha's servant.

When blind Balaam saw clearly

In Numbers 22, we read about Balaam, a misguided prophet who sought riches and honor over God's will. King Balak wanted Balaam to curse the Israelites, and even offered him a bountiful booty for the false prophetic curse. Balaam asked God about it and was told not to go. When Balak's crew upped their offer, Balaam waited on the Lord's direction. (As if God would change His mind!)

Seeing the idolatry in Balaam's heart, the Lord told him to go with Balak's men. So the prophet arose, saddled his donkey, and took off on the journey. Of course, it wasn't really the Lord's will for Balaam to curse the Israelites. God got angry that Balaam's heart was for riches and honor and sent an angel to take a stand in his path and prevent him from moving ahead. Balaam couldn't see it, but his faithful donkey could.

> Then the LORD opened the eyes of Balaam, and he saw the angel of the LORD standing in the way, and His sword was drawn in His hand, and he bowed his head and fell flat on his face. The angel of the LORD said to him, "Why have you struck your donkey these three

> times? I have come out to oppose you, because your way is perverse before Me."
>
> —Numbers 22:31–32

Now Balaam had a decision to make. Ultimately, even though the will of the Lord was made abundantly clear to him, the false prophet betrayed Israel. Mercy to the one who deliberately opposes the Lord's will after his eyes have been opened to the supernatural! It took some time, but the soothsayer fell at the sword of the children of Israel in battle (Josh. 13:22).

When Elisha's servant saw reinforcements

In Elisha's day, the king of Syria was warring against Israel. The prophet Elisha gave the Israelites a marked advantage—he was able to hear the words Syria's king spoke in his bedroom and relayed them to the king of Israel (2 Kings 6:12). The Syrian king wanted Elisha stopped, and he sent out horses and chariots and a great army to fetch him. When he saw the Syrian army surrounding the city, Elisha's servant got scared.

> When a servant of the man of God rose early in the morning and went out, a force surrounded the city both with horses and chariots. And his servant said to him, "Alas, my master! What will we do?" And he said, "Do not be afraid, for there are more with us than with them." Then Elisha prayed, "Lord, open his eyes and let him see." So the Lord opened the eyes of the young man, and he saw that the mountain was full of horses and chariots of fire surrounding Elisha.
>
> —2 Kings 6:15–17

What confidence Elisha's servant must have gained—not just in that moment but throughout his walk with the Lord.

Praying Paul's prayer

And that brings me to Paul's prayer for the church at Ephesus, which is something I would suggest praying over yourself daily. In this prayer, Paul asks the Lord to open the believers' eyes for a specific purpose—a purpose that is sure to spark faith in soul and spirit:

> Therefore I also, after hearing of your faith in the Lord Jesus and your love toward all the saints, do not cease giving thanks for you, mentioning you in my prayers, so that the God of our Lord Jesus Christ, the Father of glory, may give you the Spirit of wisdom and revelation in the knowledge of Him, that the eyes of your understanding may be enlightened, that you may know what is the hope of His calling and what are the riches of the glory of His inheritance among the saints, and what is the surpassing greatness of His power toward us who believe, according to the working of His mighty power.
>
> —Ephesians 1:15–19

Powerful!

Again, although we should not seek supernatural experiences for the sake of seeking supernatural experiences—we should seek God, and He will give us what we need—there is nothing wrong with crying out to God to open your eyes when you sense that you aren't seeing what He really wants you to see. We all have blind spots, either personally or with spiritual warfare. So cry out to God. Ask Him to flood your heart with light—to open your eyes—and to show you what He wants you to see.

A Warning About Prophetic Visions

Two words of caution about visions—and these apply equally to dreams: judge the vision and pray it through to be sure that you have the correct interpretation before trying to build a prophetic warfare strategy on it. Let me write that again: judge the vision and pray it through to be sure that you have the correct interpretation before trying to build a prophetic warfare strategy on it.

Some people confuse soulish imaginations and an active thought life for visions. The Spirit and the Word agree. If your vision doesn't line up with the Spirit or the Word, set it aside and quit meditating on it. It is more difficult to receive clear instructions from the Holy Spirit when you allow your soulish man to dominate your spirit man. The Holy Spirit communicates to your spirit man, not to your flesh or your soul.

The writer of Hebrews says this: "For the word of God is alive, and active, and sharper than any two-edged sword, piercing even to the division of soul and spirit, of joints and marrow, and able to judge the thoughts and intents of the heart" (Heb. 4:12). I love prophetic visions that come from God's heart, but I am quick to reject prophetic visions that come from man's soul. Visions of prophetic warfare strategies that don't originate from the Spirit of God will not simply fail to lead you into victory, but they could lead you into a level of spiritual warfare for which you are not prepared.

If you want nuts and bolts on interpreting visions, there are a few nuggets in chapter 5—and there are many books on the topic. James Goll's *Dream Language: The Prophetic Power of Dreams* is one I recommend. Once you have judged the vision to be from God and you have its interpretation, ask God for the timing and specific execution of the implementation. Are you supposed to do this alone? Is it a corporate strategy? Is there a time and place you should do this? Remember, the Holy Spirit that opened your eyes to the vision is the same One who will give you marching orders into victory. Listen to the Holy Ghost!

Chapter 7

THE POWER OF PROPHETIC DECLARATIONS, DECREES, AND PROCLAMATIONS

You've probably never heard a president in your lifetime proclaim a national day of fasting, humiliation, and prayer—but it was quite common in the early days of our nation. See, they were living in times of war and crisis and they understood the power of a proclamation in the spirit realm.

The Assembly of Virginia proclaimed a day of fasting, humiliation, and prayer in 1774 after the British Parliament ordered an embargo at Boston.[1] They stopped everything they were doing for an entire day to seek God with fasting and prayer. In 1776, the Continental Congress declared their allegiance to the living God.[2]

History knows well Abraham Lincoln's Emancipation Proclamation that set slaves free. In modern times, we have seen presidents make decrees that changed the nation. Franklin D. Roosevelt signed a decree that approved the Social Security Act. John F. Kennedy signed a declaration that the government would give NASA the resources to send a man to the moon. And Lyndon B. Johnson signed a decree called the Civil Rights Act.

Each of these declarations, decrees, and proclamations served a different purpose. Some were warfare strategies. Some were pleas for God's intervention in crisis. Some set the captives free. And some declared the impossible could be possible. These are natural examples, but the power of declarations, decrees, and proclamations in the spirit realm is even more powerful than it is in the natural realm.

There is power in the Word of God and in its declarations, decrees, and proclamations. Heaven and Earth will pass away, but His Word never will (Matt. 24:35). His Word is life to all those who find it, and healing to the flesh (Prov. 4:22). His Word will add length to your life and give you peace (Prov. 3:1–2). The grass withers and the flowers fade away, but the Word of God will stand forever (Isa. 40:8). His Word is spirit and life (John 6:63). His Word is truth (John 17:17). His Word is pure, like silver tried in a furnace, purified seven times (Ps. 12:6).

The Word of God Is Alive

As much as I love all of those scriptures, there are two passages in particular that are especially powerful in any discussion of declarations, decrees, and proclamations. The first one is Hebrews 4:11–16:

> Let us labor therefore to enter that rest, lest anyone fall by the same pattern of unbelief.
>
> For the word of God is alive, and active, and sharper than any two-edged sword, piercing even to the division of soul and spirit, of joints and marrow, and able to judge the thoughts and intents of the heart. There is no creature that is not revealed in His sight, for all things are bare and exposed to the eyes of Him to whom we must give account.
>
> Since then we have a great High Priest who has passed into the heavens, Jesus the Son of God, let us hold firmly to our confession. For we do not have a High Priest who cannot sympathize with our weaknesses, but One who

> was in every sense tempted like we are, yet without sin. Let us then come with confidence to the throne of grace, that we may obtain mercy and find grace to help in time of need."

In this passage, the writer of Hebrews warns us against not believing God's Word. He explains that the Word of God is alive. The word *alive* in that verse is the Greek word *zao*. According to *The KJV New Testament Greek Lexicon*, some of its definitions are "to live, breathe, to be among the living (not lifeless, not dead); living water, having vital power in itself and exerting the same upon the soul." The Amplified Bible, Classic Edition says God's Word is "alive and full of power [making it active, operative, energizing, and effective]."

Jesus is alive. Jesus is the Word made flesh. Therefore it only stands to reason that the Word of God is alive. When you proclaim the Word of God over your life, the Holy Spirit can breathe on a situation. The writer of Hebrews calls God's Word powerful. When you declare the Word during spiritual warfare, it has vital power to bring itself to pass. In other words, the power necessary to accomplish God's declared Word is contained in the Word itself. Words are like containers of power, and they carry the power of death and life (Prov. 18:21).

But that's not all. The Word of God is also sharp. In fact, it is sharper than any two-edged sword. That means your sword of the Spirit, which is the Word of God, can cut through any weapon that is formed against you. That is why God can so confidently declare that those weapons cannot prosper. This truth is part of our spiritual heritage (Is. 54:17). Finally, God's Word pierces, or penetrates, the darkness. The unfolding of His Word gives light (Ps. 119:130), and darkness has to flee when that Word is declared in faith. The Father of lights enforces His Word.

God's Word is also a discerner or judge. We need the discerning of spirits in our prophetic warfare battle chest, and the Word is one of our primary weapons. Even if you don't operate in the gift of discerning spirits, you can rely on the Word of God to do the judging for you. The key is to be led forth by the Spirit of God in choosing which scriptures you battle with. The Word alone will work, but when you tap into the prophetic Holy Spirit to use the right scripture at the right time, you can often end the battle with one swing of the sword.

On the other hand, when you are waging prophetic warfare, the onslaught can seem overwhelming at times. Your arms can grow weary from swinging the sword and keeping your shield of faith high at the same time. I have wanted to quit and give up more times than I am willing to admit—but I never did because Jesus didn't. The passage of Scripture in Hebrews 4:11–16 tells us to hold firmly to our confession. In this context you could just as easily say to hold fast to your proclamation, your decree, or your declaration. Sometimes it takes more than one swing of the sword. Don't give up. The Word of God never fails.

God's Word Always Accomplishes Its Goal

I am very goal-oriented. Some call me driven. At the beginning of each year, I prayerfully write out goals for the year ahead—spiritual goals and natural goals. I then break those goals down by month, then by week, and then by day. I am essentially taking a page right out of Habakkuk 2:2: "Write the vision, and make it plain on tablets, that he who reads it may run."

At the end of each year I look back at the goals I have accomplished, and it encourages my heart. I don't always hit them all, but I make a lot of progress and I give God all the glory. Now, of course, God always accomplishes His goals. His

Word always does what He intends for it to do. It never fails. If God says it, that settles it. Numbers 23:19 assures us, "God is not a man, that He should lie, nor a son of man, that He should repent. Has He spoken, and will He not do it? Or has He spoken, and will He not make it good?"

Aren't you glad? With that in mind, here is the second passage that is especially powerful in any discussion of declarations, decrees, and proclamations:

> For My thoughts are not your thoughts, nor are your ways My ways, says the LORD. For as the heavens are higher than the earth, so are My ways higher than your ways, and My thoughts than your thoughts. For as the rain comes down, and the snow from heaven, and do not return there but water the earth and make it bring forth and bud that it may give seed to the sower and bread to the eater, so shall My word be that goes forth from My mouth; it shall not return to Me void, but it shall accomplish that which I please, and it shall prosper in the thing for which I sent it.
>
> —ISAIAH 55:8–11

If you can get this revelation, you will walk in much more victory in every area of your life. These verses stir a war cry in my spirit. Although the Lord wasn't speaking to Isaiah in the context of warfare, these verses nevertheless apply to waging prophetic warfare. What is true about His Word in one setting is true about His Word in another setting. His Word does not change whether you apply it to healing, financial issues, relationship troubles, or spiritual warfare. And, I submit to you, the devil is in the mix with many health, financial, and relationship troubles.

Let's break this down. First of all, God's thoughts are higher than our thoughts. Since the battle is against the mind, and our weapons of warfare are not carnal but mighty through

God to pull down strongholds, we need to tap into God's thoughts. Many of God's thoughts are in the Scripture.

Of course, God can also speak His thoughts to us prophetically over a specific situation. God told Jeremiah: "Call to Me, and I will answer you, and show you great and mighty things which you do not know" (Jer. 33:3). Many times, in the heat of the battle, we need to call on God for some great and mighty things we don't know. Much the same, His ways are higher than our ways. We can get into a spiritual warfare rut, binding and loosing the same five devils no matter what comes against us. That is ineffective. God wants to prophetically show you the way to victory, but you have to let Him—and it may not be the way you think.

The Lord makes a natural comparison in Isaiah 55 that is helpful to understand. The rain comes down, but it doesn't go back up from the dark clouds, right? The snow comes down, but it melts on the ground rather than going back to the sky. They have a purpose—to water the earth. If the rain and snow returned to the sky, they would not fulfill their purpose but would leave the earth dry and therefore barren. God's Word is just like that.

The Lord says, "So shall My word be that goes forth from My mouth; it shall not return to Me void, but it shall accomplish that which I please, and it shall prosper in the thing for which I sent it" (Isa. 55:11). That word *void* is worth exploring. It comes from the Hebrew word *reyqam*, which means "vainly, emptily; in an empty condition; in vain, without effect." Essentially, something that is void is useless. It makes no impact. Think of a voided check. You can't use it for anything valuable. God's Word carries weight. True prophetic words carry weight.

When you proclaim, decree, and declare God's Word over a situation, you had better believe it's going to accomplish what it was sent to do. It might not look like it is accomplishing much immediately, but it is dynamic in its power and will push back darkness. When we proclaim, decree, and declare God's Word—written or prophetic—we can be sure something is happening in the spirit realm. It may not happen as quickly as we like—or it may happen immediately. I prefer the immediately scenario, but I have learned to endure.

Dealing With Prophetic Decrees

We have been talking largely about the written Word of God, but all of this applies equally to tried and true prophetic words. If God speaks to your heart and gives you a strategy, the words He speaks to you are just as active and alive and sharp as Scripture. They are still God's words. Let's dive into prophetic decrees.

Simply stated, a *decree* is "an order usually having the force of law," according to *Merriam-Webster*.[3] God expects us to follow His decrees (Lev. 18:4). The enemy is also bound to obey a prophetic declaration in the name of Jesus, the name at which every knee must bow and every tongue confess that He is Lord (Rom. 14:11). We read about kings in the Old Testament making decrees: King Cyrus made a decree to rebuild the house of God (Ezra 5:13).

The Bible calls us kings and priests to our God, and we shall reign on the earth (Rev. 5:10). It's up to us to do it. Jesus told us to "occupy till I come" (Luke 19:13, KJV). Job 22:28 says, "Thou shalt also decree a thing, and it shall be established unto thee: and the light shall shine upon thy ways" (KJV).

When it comes to waging prophetic warfare, our Spirit-led decrees have the force of law behind them. We can decree God's statutes, doctrines, judgments, thoughts, ways, ordinances, laws, rules, and the like prophetically. We can speak those things that are not as though they were until we see them manifest in the natural realm (Rom. 4:17).

We can prophetically declare that our nation is one under God in agreement with our Founding Fathers. We can prophetically declare that our marriages will remain strong in agreement with Matthew 19:6. We can prophetically declare that our children will not stray from the Lord when they grow old in agreement with Proverbs 22:6. And we can also prophetically decree anything the Lord tells us to by His Spirit.

I went to Florida's capitol building in Tallahassee with a group of intercessors to make prophetic decrees over our state. See, the government of the earth is really taking place in prayer. We decreed revival in our state. We decreed an end to racism in our state. We decreed godly leaders in our state. We decreed a strong economy in our state. We worshipped and prayed and decreed and declared for a couple of hours, and I know that those declarations were not empty because they were not a rote religious practice. They were inspired prophetically by God.

Be sensitive to God's inspiration. A friend of mine was grieved when she discovered the city of Deerfield Beach decided to erect replicas of Easter Island-style statues in the Atlantic Ocean near her home. These were ugly statues that looked something like what I imagine the idol Dagon looked like.

God had been revealing to her heart the need to "speak to things." So she decreed that these idols would not be planted in the ocean to form a 150-foot barrage but that they would fall, in the name of Jesus. To her delight, newspapers in South Florida told the story of a top-heavy barge that flipped over and landed on top of the statues. The statues were crushed. That decree reminded me of a passage in 1 Samuel 5:1–5:

> Now the Philistines took the ark of God, and brought it from Ebenezer to Ashdod. When the Philistines took the ark of God, they brought it into the house of Dagon and set it by Dagon. When the Ashdodites arose early

> in the morning, Dagon had fallen upon his face to the ground before the ark of the LORD. And they took Dagon and set him in his place again. When they arose early on the next morning, again Dagon was fallen upon his face to the ground before the ark of the LORD, and the head of Dagon and both the palms of his hands were cut off upon the threshold. Only the torso of Dagon was left to him. Therefore neither the priests of Dagon, nor any coming into Dagon's house, tread on the threshold of Dagon in Ashdod to this day.

MAKING PROPHETIC DECLARATIONS

You can make prophetic decrees over your life, family, ministry, business, or anything else God speaks to you about with authority—and you should. You can also make declarations, which are similar but somewhat different. You can make a decree privately, but declarations are public by nature. You might say a decree is an order and a declaration is the announcement of it.

Merriam-Webster defines *declare* as "to make known formally, officially, or explicitly."[4] And a *declaration* is "the act of declaring: announcement; the first pleading in a common-law action; a statement made by a party to a legal transaction usually not under oath; something that is declared; a document containing such a declaration."[5]

We are called to declare the works of the Lord (Ps. 118:17). His name shall be declared throughout all the earth (Exod. 9:16), as well as "His glory among the nations, His wonders among all the peoples" (1 Chron. 16:24). Moses declared laws (Deut. 1:5). The Israelites declared peace (Judg. 21:13). Once, the Lord declared disaster over the wicked king Ahab (2 Chron. 18:22).

We can declare the written Word of God or the prophetic word of God. When Peter declared that Jesus was the Son of

God, the Lord said that flesh and blood did not reveal that declaration to him (Matt. 16:13–17); Father God in heaven downloaded that revelation into Peter's spirit. Later on in this chapter I will show you how to develop declarations using the Word of God.

A prophetic declaration may be different. It may be a *rhema* word from Scripture—a verse from the Bible that God illuminates in your spirit—or it could be a direct revelation from the Spirit about a specific situation. It could be a word of wisdom, a word of knowledge, or a prophecy on which you base your declaration in the context of warfare.

We hosted Ron Teal for the School of the Prophets at my home base of Awakening House of Prayer in South Florida. During his visit Ron made a prophetic declaration that this house would be known as a house of the supernatural, where signs, wonders, and miracles happen. Two weeks later we held our first women's conference. I had an unction to call for healing. I hesitated and asked the Lord what He wanted to heal: necks, backs, knees, cancer? He said, "I want to heal it all." So I made a general call for healing, and thirty-two women were healed by the power of God. But Ron made the prophetic declaration before the well opened up.

THE POWER OF PROPHETIC PROCLAMATIONS

Although it is similar in nature, proclaiming goes a little further than declaring. *Merriam-Webster* defines *proclaim* as "to say or state (something) in a public, official, or definite way: to declare or announce (something); to show (something) clearly."[6] That something, in our case, is God's will.

It follows then that *proclamation* is defined as "the act of saying something in a public, official, or definite way: the act of proclaiming something; an official statement or announcement made by a person in power or by a government."[7] You are the person in power in the government of God in the name of Jesus. Jesus gave us authority over serpents and scorpions and all the power of the enemy (Luke 10:19–20). He expects you to make proclamations to establish His kingdom on earth. We are first and foremost to proclaim the name of the Lord (Deut. 32:3). In other words, we are called to make His name known.

In Old Testament times, the Israelites proclaimed a Jubilee every fifty years (Lev. 25:10). It was a supernatural debt cancellation and the setting free of captives. That is the kind of proclamation I love to hear! Samuel had the sad task of proclaiming judgment in Israel, as did many other Old Testament prophets.

Again, we will look at how to form prophetic proclamations in just a moment. But I want to focus on another aspect of war proclamations before we go there. On November 1, 1777, the Continental Congress made a proclamation to seek God in a time of war. This should be our first proclamation before entering the spiritual battlefield. Here is a portion of this famous proclamation:

> That with one Heart and one Voice the good People may express the grateful Feelings of their Hearts, and consecrate themselves to the Service of their Divine Benefactor; and that together with their sincere Acknowledgments and Offerings, they may join the penitent Confession of their manifold Sins, whereby they had forfeited every Favour, and their humble and earnest Supplication that it may please GOD, through the Merits of Jesus Christ, mercifully to forgive and blot them out of Remembrance; That it may please him graciously to afford his Blessing on the Governments of these States respectively, and prosper the public Council of the whole; to inspire our Commanders both by Land and Sea, and all under them, with that Wisdom and Fortitude which may render

> them fit Instruments, under the Providence of Almighty GOD, to secure for these United States the greatest of all human blessings, INDEPENDENCE and PEACE.[8]

We need God's help every step of the way. We have His authority, but we need to exercise it rightly. We don't want to buffet the air. We need His prophetic insight, His unction, and His leading to gain a swift victory. Worshipping before you go to war will bring stronger results.

Creating Prophetic Proclamations, Decrees, and Declarations

As I have said throughout this chapter, we can decree, declare, and proclaim God's Word, but when we have a prophetic unction—when God gives us a declaration—it becomes a powerful spiritual warfare strategy. Whether it's a scripture the Holy Spirit illuminates as a prophetic decree or declaration, or a prophetic word He releases through us, decrees, declarations, and proclamations carry power and authority to overcome the enemy.

You have heard many times that the power of death and life is in the tongue (Prov. 18:21). You will eat the fruit of your lips (Prov. 13:2). I believe strongly in praying the Word and confessing the Word because God's Word is God's will. You can't go wrong praying and confessing God's Word. But we can also declare, decree, and proclaim it. And we can do this with the written Word of God or a prophetic word of God judged true. It is, of course, important to judge prophetic words before you decide to pray them out or declare and decree them. You can learn more about how to judge prophecy in my book *Did The Spirit of God Say That?*

First let's create a prophetic warfare declaration from the Word of God using Isaiah 54:17, which reads: "No weapon that is formed against you shall prosper, and every tongue that shall rise against you in judgment, you shall condemn. This is the heritage of the servants of the LORD, and their vindication is from Me, says the LORD."

This is one of my favorite warfare declarations. If I am praying it for myself, I personalize it. "I decree and declare that no weapon formed against me shall prosper, and every tongue that shall rise against me in judgment, I shall condemn. This is the heritage of the servants of the Lord, and my vindication is from You, Lord." You can do this with any scripture and be on safe ground.

You can't go wrong decreeing, declaring, and proclaiming the Word of God. Your faith will rise, though, if it is a *rhema* word of God, meaning a word God speaks to your heart. It can be a scripture from the Bible that really hits your spirit or comes to your mind during warfare, or it can be a prophetic word. Remember, Jesus said, "Man shall not live by bread alone, but by every word that proceeds out of the mouth of God" (Matt. 4:4). Words are still proceeding out of God's mouth, and we are to live by and war with them.

I was once in a spiritual war over a condo I was trying to purchase. The situation looked fairly hopeless. The devil was doing everything he could to stop the deal. It fell through three times. Thankfully, I had a prophetic word from God. He spoke a word to my heart in line with Jeremiah 32:10. The Lord told me, "The deed is signed." I decreed and declared that Word until the enemy backed off.

In 2001, during a massive trial in my life, the Holy Spirit spoke to me in an audible voice and said, "Stay calm. Be patient. Your time is coming." I decreed, declared, proclaimed, and rested in that word through the good times and the bad—and the warfare. Write down the prophetic words you receive. They may come to you in the midst of the battle, or they may be spoken to you in the middle of the night for use in a future battle. In the next chapter we will explore the world of prophetic acts.

Chapter 8

EXECUTING SPIRIT-INSPIRED PROPHETIC ACTS

Window Rock, Arizona—it's a small city and the governmental capital of the Navajo Nation. The Navajo Nation is the largest territory of a sovereign Native American nation in North America. It is called Window Rock because the major landmark in the city is a massive rock with a hole through the middle, like a window.[1]

But Window Rock is more than a famous landmark—it is also one of four places where the Navajo medicine men carry their woven water jugs to gather water for a ceremony during which they ask false gods for rain.[2] Indeed, Window Rock is a site marked by the medicine men's witchcraft. A local told me there were demons stationed around the famed rock and that anyone who got too close came under fierce attack.

Of course, I didn't know that last part when we set out to do a prophetic act at the rock with a hole through it. See, the Navajo Nation has serious water supply issues. According to the nonprofit DigDeep, if you are born Navajo, you are sixty-seven times more likely not to have a tap or toilet in your house than other Americans.[3]

On top of that, the suicide rate among Native American adults grew 65.2 percent from 1999 to 2010, according to the Centers for Disease Control.[4] The Department of Justice reveals Native Americans are 2.5 times more likely to be sexually assaulted than other Americans.[5] Poverty, unemployment, low graduation rates, debilitating diseases, cardiovascular disease, obesity, and alcoholism plague the Navajo Nation.

The medicine men and their witchcraft don't seem to be curing anything that ails the Navajo Nation. That is why our apostolic team decided to obey the Holy Spirit and break the curse of the nation. We headed out to Window Rock, and a small group from our team beelined for the rock with a hole through it. The only problem was the chain-link fence in between us and the epicenter.

When I failed to squeeze through the five-inch opening between the fence and rock, two of the apostles hoisted me over the wall with a prayer cloth and clear instructions to break curses and release healing. So there I stood, one small speck against a massive orange rock background, standing in the gap for a nation in crisis, crying out to the Lord to break in with light, and blessing a people who have lived under a curse for hundreds of years. I tucked the anointed prayer cloth tightly in the cleft of a rock and made my way back over the fence, surprisingly without ripping my jeans.

Within three months we started seeing the early fruit of this prophetic act. The Navajo Nation launched a nationwide search for a police chief after being without one for several years.[6] Navajo Nation schools received $45 million in federal funding that had been held up for twelve years.[7] Wholesome Wave and the Navajo Nation have partnered to increase access to healthy foods.[8] A Navajo judge was convicted of abusing his office by showing favor to defendants—members of his family—in a burglary investigation.[9] The Navajo Nation closed its first ever bond transaction, selling nearly $53 million of investment-grade tax-exempt bonds to fund infrastructure projects.[10] And the list goes on.

We are not presuming to say that this one prophetic act set all of these blessings in motion. We are one of many groups that visit the Navajo Nation, and the Navajo Nation is home to many strong churches that pray without ceasing. But we do believe we played a part in pushing back some of the darkness that is invading the lives of these precious people. The job is not done. More intercession is needed. More warfare needs to be waged. But this one prophetic act contributed some color to the bigger picture.

What Is a Prophetic Act?

My story about the Navajo Nation illustrated a prophetic act, but let's define the concept more precisely before we go any deeper. My simple definition of a *prophetic act* is "an action God asks you to take in order to illustrate a principle or act out His will in a situation." At Window Rock I made prophetic declarations and left an anointed prayer cloth in the cleft of a rock to break the yoke of bondage.

In his best-selling book *Intercessory Prayer*, Dutch Sheets explains:

> Prophetic action or declaration is something said or done in the natural realm at the direction of God that prepares the way for Him to move in the spiritual realm, which then consequently effects change in the natural realm...God says to do or say something. We obey. Our words or actions impact the heavenly realm, which then impacts the natural realm.[11]

Barbara Wentroble, author of *Prophetic Intercession*, defines a *prophetic act* as "a thing or deed done, having the powers of a prophet; an action or decree that predicts or foreshadows,"[12] while Chuck Pierce defines a *prophetic act* as "a physical act performed at the prompting of the Lord that illustrates something the Lord is speaking prophetically into a situation" in his book *The Future War of the Church: How We Can Defeat Lawlessness and Bring God's Order to Earth.*[13]

Cindy Jacobs, cofounder of Generals International, says as a person is trained to prophesy, the Lord will often work intensively in the area of obedience. "There are special strategic 'windows of time' to not only pray, but also to obey by doing a physical act that might be called an intercessory act or a prophetic act," she writes in her book *The Voice of God: How God Speaks Personally and Corporately to His Children Today.* "At times, such acts may seem a bit unusual but can be powerful in breaking down strongholds."[14]

The Bible is full of prophetic acts, which should give us a clue as to one of the important ways God likes to use people in the earth realm as a point of contact through intercessory prayer and action in spiritual warfare. First, let me point out that all prophetic acts don't relate to spiritual warfare. Prophetic acts can be used to bring a warning, to announce a call into ministry, to facilitate healing, and much more. (See Ezekiel 4–5; 1 Kings 19:19; and 2 Kings 5:9–14) But prophetic acts can also be especially strategic in spiritual warfare. As you read some examples from the pages of the Bible, ask the Lord to open your eyes and ears to His leading and guiding in the realm of prophetic acts.

Moses and his intercessors battle in prayer

Moses did his fair share of prophetic acts. He held out his rod and God parted the Red Sea so the Israelites could escape the raging Egyptian army (Exod. 14:21). He struck a rock with his rod and water came out so the people could drink (Exod. 17:6). And right after that he engaged in a team prophetic act in Israel's battle against the Amalekites. We read about this in Exodus 17:8–13:

> Then Amalek came and fought with Israel in Rephidim. So Moses said to Joshua, "Choose men for us and go out, fight against Amalek. Tomorrow I will stand on the top of the hill with the rod of God in my hand."
>
> So Joshua did as Moses had said to him and fought against Amalek. And Moses, Aaron, and Hur went up to the top of the hill. Now when Moses held up his hand, Israel prevailed, but when he let down his hand, Amalek prevailed. But Moses' hands became heavy. So they took a stone, and put it under him, and he sat on it. And Aaron and Hur supported his hands, one on one side, and the other on the other side. And his hands were steady until the going down of the sun. So Joshua laid low Amalek and his people with the edge of the sword.

Matthew Henry's commentary suggests that Moses's wonder-working rod was a prophetic symbol to the nation of Israel but that it was also an appeal to heaven. "Moses was not only a standard-bearer, but an intercessor, pleading with God for success and victory."[15]

Prophetic actions can determine the outcome of spiritual warfare

In 2 Kings, an especially prophetic chapter of the Bible, we learn the importance of obeying prophetic acts—and exercising them to the fullest. In this scene, Elisha was sick with the illness from which he would die. Joash, the reigning king of Israel, went down to visit him, weeping, and received a strategic prophetic word. We read about this account in 2 Kings 13:15–17:

> Elisha said to him, "Take a bow and arrows." So he took a bow and arrows. Then he said to the king of Israel, "Draw the bow." So he drew it. Elisha put his hands on the king's hands.

> Then he said, "Open the east window." So he opened it. Then Elisha said, "Shoot." So he shot. Then he said, "The arrow of the deliverance of the LORD, and the arrow of deliverance from Aram; for you must strike Aram in Aphek until you have destroyed them."

That is tragic, but it demonstrates how serious we need to take prophetic acts. If it were me, I would have struck the ground until my arms were too weak to keep striking—and then I would have handed the bow and arrow to another intercessor to continue the strike. Here is the lesson: when God reveals a prophetic act, be sure that you complete the act.

How will you know when you have completed the act? Some prophetic acts have a clear end and beginning—put this anointed prayer cloth in the cleft of a rock in the Navajo Nation. But with other prophetic acts, you have to continue until you feel a ring of victory or release in your spirit. The God who assigned you the prophetic act will make it clear when the act has accomplished His purposes in the spirit. That doesn't mean you will always see immediate results in the natural, but you can have peace knowing that you have done your part and God will do His part.

Taking down an army with prophetic acts

Israel was fighting more than pests in its crops—it was fighting enemy arms that would rise up against them and decimate the food supply. The Bible says these enemies did not leave any provisions (no sheep, cattle, or donkeys); they swarmed in like locusts to destroy the land (Judg. 6:3–5). We see the prophetic act that brought victory in Judges 7:19–22:

> So Gideon and a hundred men with him went to the edge of the camp at the start of the middle night watch, just as they were setting the watch. Then they blew the horns and smashed the jars in their hands. The three

> combat units blew the horns and broke the jars. They held the torches in their left hands and the horns for blowing in their right hands. They called out, "A sword for the LORD and for Gideon!" Every man stood in his place all around the camp, but the men in the camp ran, shouted, and fled.
>
> When they blew the three hundred horns, the LORD turned every man's sword against his fellow man throughout the camp. The Midianite camp fled to Beth Shittah in the direction of Zererah, up to the border of Abel Meholah, near Tabbath.

Who would think blowing horns and smashing jars would bring victory? Prophetic acts don't always make sense to the mind. In fact, many times prophetic acts defy reasoning. But we walk by faith and not by sight (2 Cor. 5:7). We also prophesy according to the proportion of our faith (Rom. 12:6). And that includes prophetic acts. Indeed, it takes faith to execute prophetic acts. Imagine lying on your left side for 390 days to bear the iniquity of Israel, then turning over on your right side for 40 days to bear the iniquity of Judah (Ezek. 4). No one would do such a thing if they didn't have great faith.

True prophetic words can combat false prophetic acts

Micaiah stood against false prophetic acts in his day. Ahab, the king of Israel, and Jehoshaphat, the king of Judah, gathered the prophets of the land to prophesy to them about going to battle against Ramoth Gilead. In a prophetic act, a false prophet named Zedekiah made horns of iron and said, "Thus says the LORD: With these you shall push the Arameans until you have consumed them" (1 Kings 22:11). That sparked more false prophecies that agreed with Zedekiah. Then uncompromising Micaiah came on the scene. We read about the prophetic showdown in 1 Kings 22:17–24:

> And he said, "I saw all Israel scattered upon the hills, as sheep without a shepherd, and the LORD said, 'These have no master. Let every man return to his own house in peace.'"
>
> The king of Israel said to Jehoshaphat, "Did I not tell you that he would not prophesy good concerning me, but evil?"
>
> And he said, "Hear, therefore, the word of the LORD: I saw the LORD sitting on His throne, and all the host of heaven standing beside Him on His right hand and on His left. The LORD said, 'Who will persuade Ahab so that he will go up and die at Ramoth Gilead?'
>
> "And one said this, and another said that. Then a spirit came forth and stood before the LORD and said, 'I will persuade him.'
>
> "The LORD said to him, 'How?'
>
> "And he said, 'I will go and be a lying spirit in the mouth of all his prophets.'
>
> "And He said, 'You will be successful and persuade him. Go forth, and do so.'
>
> "Now therefore, the LORD has put a lying spirit in the mouths of all your prophets here, and He has spoken evil concerning you!"
>
> Then Zedekiah the son of Kenaanah walked up and struck Micaiah on the cheek and said, "Which way did the spirit of the LORD go from me in order to speak to you?"

Micaiah revealed the truth, but Ahab and Jehoshaphat decided to go to war with Ramoth Gilead anyway. Ahab died in the heat of the battle as a result—but he had been warned. God, in His mercy, sent a true prophetic act to combat the false prophetic warfare act.

The Isaiah 22:22 Prophetic Act That Breaks Down Barriers

Jesus gave us the keys to the kingdom. Whatever we bind on earth shall be bound in heaven, and whatever we loose on earth shall be loosed in heaven (Matt. 16:19). As spiritual warriors many of us have become experts at binding and loosing. But there is another prophetic key that believers can use to open doors that no one can then shut and shut doors that no one can then open.

The Word of God reveals this prophetic key in both the Old and New Testaments. It is the key of David. Some call it the Isaiah 22:22 key, but you could also call it the Revelation 3:7 key because the prophetic scripture is mentioned in both books. Isaiah 22:22 reads, "The key of the house of David I will lay on his shoulder. Then he shall open, and no one shall shut. And he shall shut, and no one shall open."

Of course, the *he* in this verse is Jesus. Jesus has the key and can open and shut as He wills. When Jesus opens the door, no man can shut it, and when Jesus shuts the door, no man can open it. Our job as prophetic people is to discern His will and kingdom purpose so we can exercise our authority in His name to open what He wants opened and shut what He wants shut.

Again, the key is discerning His will. Jesus has not called us to be reckless with the key of David, nor will the Isaiah 22:22 key work if we try to turn it in a direction opposite His will. But when we hear from the Lord, we can turn that key with confidence and decree and declare that doors will open or close. It is a powerful prophetic act that breaks down barriers.

Here is a good example of how this works in action: Ken Malone of Forerunner Ministries ministered at my revival hub, Awakening House of Prayer. When he walked into our little prayer room, he told me it was not big enough to accommodate what God wanted to do in the ministry. Of course I agreed, but we didn't have any other open doors at the time.

What I didn't know was that he'd brought his big silver Isaiah 22:22 key and was led to unlock new property for the ministry in a prophetic act. At the end of the service the man of God brought out that key by the unction of the Holy Spirit and decreed and declared property to open up for the ministry. The authority of his words and the anointing in the room were strong.

The next week I approached the building owner about moving us into a larger spot they had in mind for us when we outgrew our current square footage. That is when I discovered something unexpected—not only was the spot unavailable, but the owners were planning to relocate us into an even smaller area. My jaw dropped.

Within three weeks they had downsized us. But also within three weeks, God opened the door to a second facility ten minutes (rather than forty-five minutes) from my home—a larger facility that was more suited to our training center. There is much more to the prophetic swirl, such as the 1948 Tyler Street address (1948 was the year Israel was reborn), the fact that the owners are Jewish and their last name is one of the names for Jesus in Scripture, and the building was a gold color just like our logo. I could go on and on with the prophetic bread crumbs.

A Governing Key of Authority

The Isaiah 22:22 key also carries a governmental authority. Through our intercession and Spirit-inspired prophetic acts, we can impact our society. God wants to bring an awakening to your city, to your state, and to your nation. I went to Florida's state capitol building in Tallahassee with a large group of people to pray over our state along those lines.

Malone brought his big silver Isaiah 22:22 key, and many of us gripped it in our hands as we decreed and declared God's will over the state. We opened the door for righteousness and closed the door to racism. We opened the door to godly government and closed the door to corruption, and more. We believe we were in God's will, and we are believing God for transforming revival in the Forerunner State.

"Some of you may be instructed of the Lord, as I have been, to use your Isaiah 22:22 key within the sphere of government, and particularly within Washington DC," says Dutch Sheets, author of *Intercessory Prayer*. "Some of you are called to pray for your state capital, your city or even another nation. Others of you may be assigned to use your kingdom keys in the financial realm, for educational institutions or for the entertainment sector. As you seek the Lord, He will reveal these and other assignments to you."[16]

A Few Cautions About Prophetic Acts

Throughout this chapter I have shared with you a handful of spiritual warfare prophetic acts in Scripture and prophetic acts I've witnessed firsthand. There are some other strange prophetic acts in Scripture that I didn't mention because they don't relate to our topic of waging prophetic warfare, like Hosea marrying a prostitute (Hosea 1:2) and Isaiah running around naked (Isa. 20).

We see in Scripture that prophetic acts can be especially strange, but we don't want to do something over-the-top odd unless we know it is the Holy Ghost moving us. Again, we prophesy according to the proportion of our faith, but we need to make sure we are sowing our faith into a valid prophetic unction.

Prophetic acts are more difficult to judge than prophetic words. Still, we must work to validate our prophetic unction before taking action. It would have been foolish, for example, to climb over a fence and break curses over Window Rock without truly knowing it was the will of the Lord. With demons stationed in the territory and clear evidence of massive retaliation against others who had done this without an unction, the fear of the Lord was sobering. We didn't take on that prophetic act lightly, and we prayed against the retaliation when we were finished.

What we do know is this: a prophetic act will never violate Scripture. In other words, the Holy Spirit will never lead you and guide you to disobey the written Word of God with a prophetic act. Never. The Holy Spirit leads us and guides us into all truth (John 16:13). He will not lead us into deception or danger.

Although a prophetic act may bring attention to us—I can imagine Ezekiel and Isaiah drew plenty of stares when executing their God-instructed prophetic acts—these expressions should ultimately exalt Jesus. All prophecy should exalt Jesus. The Holy Spirit always exalts Jesus (John 16:14). If we are engaging in a prophetic act for showmanship, we are behaving like the Pharisees who made long prayers just for show (Matt. 23:14) and loved to stand and pray in the synagogues and at the street corners so people would see them (Matt. 6:5). As we engage in prophetic acts, we need to keep our hearts free from religion.

We also need to stand against the temptation from Jezebel to control or manipulate people or situations with prophetic acts. When the prophet Agabus met Paul, he took Paul's belt and bound his own hands and feet, saying, "The Holy Spirit says, 'In this manner the Jews at Jerusalem shall bind the man who owns this belt and deliver him into the hands of the Gentiles'" (Acts 21:11). Agabus did this with a pure heart. Although Paul's team implored him not to go to Jerusalem, there is no record of Agabus trying to persuade Paul. The prophetic act served as a warning, not a directional prophecy. It is important to understand the difference and not step outside the bounds of your prophetic assignment.

Finally, understand that not all Christians will understand or agree with prophetic acts, even if they do believe in spiritual warfare. If you are among a conservative group of Christians and operating under their authority in a ministry setting, wisdom dictates submitting your prophetic unction to the leader before announcing what you feel the Lord is telling you to do. Although we don't want to quench the spirit, Paul told us everything should be done "decently and in order" (1 Cor. 14:40). If you get an unction for a prophetic act, you can always execute it at a later time rather than imposing on a ministry culture that could be offended.

CHAPTER 9

WAGING WAR WITH PROPHETIC WORDS

THE BODY OF Christ is in a season of war. As I said at the outset of this book, we have moved from peacetime Christianity to wartime Christianity in these last days. Of course, this war is not new, and the battle is the Lord's (2 Chron. 20:15). But we are His war clubs (Jer. 51:20), and He reveals His battle plans to us through prophetic words. In fact, true prophecies are a sword of the Spirit that can cut through enemy opposition in our lives, our families, our cities, and our nations.

I am a big proponent of pressing into the Holy Spirit for battle plans. While spiritual warfare scriptures—like putting on the whole armor of God (Eph. 6) or casting down imaginations (2 Cor. 10:5)—are always true all the time, I believe certain weapons and certain strategies are most appropriate at certain times.

For example, God once told Joshua to have men of fighting age march around the city once a day for six days, then march around the city seven times on the seventh day with the priests blowing the trumpets, and then let out a battle cry on the last long blast (Josh. 6). That strategy brought the walls of Jericho tumbling down, but it is not the right strategy for every battle.

Indeed, we see many warfare strategies in Scripture. The key is to discern and execute the warfare strategy God is breathing on during any given season and for specific situations. In this season I believe there is Holy Spirit wind on a strategy Paul gave his spiritual son Timothy: "This command I commit to you, my son Timothy, according to the prophecies that were previously given to you, that by them you might fight a good fight" (1 Tim. 1:18).

Understanding the Purpose of Prophetic Words

Let me step back a moment and offer some basics on personal prophetic words. In its simplest terms a prophecy is a promise from God. A prophecy expresses the desire and will of God over a person, place, or situation. Some prophecies are unconditional—the end-times prophecies will come to pass no matter what we do or don't do. But some prophecies are conditional; for these, God is willing to do His part, but we have to do our part.

Most personal prophecy is conditional. We have to cooperate with God to see His will come to pass. For example, if God calls you as a missionary to China, you need to prepare your heart through prayer, but you also need to do some practical things, such as get a passport, learn the Chinese language, and study the culture. If He has called you to start a business, you need to make a business plan, perhaps get a business license, and probably raise funding. Prayer is vital, but faith without works is dead (James 2:17).

Praying out the prophecies you have received is a keen strategy from the Bible, but you should not start praying out prophecies that have not first been judged. I write about this topic extensively in my book *Did the Spirit of God Say That?* In general though, prophetic words can be traced back to any one of three sources:

1. Prophecy can come from your human spirit. Jeremiah 23:16 declares, "Do not listen to the

words of the prophets who prophesy to you. They lead you into vanity; they speak a vision of their own heart and not out of the mouth of the LORD."

2. Prophecy can come from an evil spirit. In fact, the devil prophesies to you all the time. It is called vain imaginations. People can tap into the spirit of witchcraft, a familiar spirit, the Jezebel spirit, the spirit of Baal, or some other spirit. Jeremiah 23:13 reveals, "I have seen the folly in the prophets of Samaria. They prophesied by Baal and caused My people Israel to err."
3. Prophecy can come from the Holy Spirit. This is the only true source of prophecy. What you prophesy out of your spirit may even be good and edifying—but that doesn't mean it is from God. Peter reveals, "For no prophecy at any time was produced by the will of man, but holy men moved by the Holy Spirit spoke from God" (2 Pet. 1:21).

We find the purpose of the simple gift of prophecy in 1 Corinthians 14:3: "But he who prophesies speaks to men for their edification and exhortation and comfort."

The word *edification* in this scripture comes from the Greek word *oikodome*, which means "to build up, establish, strengthen, to make effective."[1] *Exhortation* in this verse is rooted in the Greek word *paraklesis*, which means "a comforting encouragement provided in times of disappointment and affliction resulting in strengthening the resolve of the believer."[2] And *comfort* stems from the Greek word *paramuthia*, which means "to provide a freedom from worry during times of grief, affliction or distress and bringing assurance to the believer."[3]

Although there are corrective prophecies, warning prophecies, and directional prophecies that may lead you into warfare over your cities and regions, personal prophecy follows the 1 Corinthians 14:3 guideline and therefore should not breed fear, confusion, or other ungodly fruit. Prophecy ultimately exalts Jesus because we know "the testimony of Jesus is the spirit of prophecy" (Rev. 19:10).

Prophecy can warn you of what the enemy is planning, help you understand the times and seasons, lift you up when you feel down, offer direction for your life, or announce a gift or calling—but it will never violate Scripture or lead you away from Christ. You don't want to put your faith in—or pray through—a prophecy that did not come from the heart of God. If you are not sure if a prophecy is accurate, continue praying and asking God for confirmation, and submit it to prophetic elders who can help you judge it. Ultimately though, you need to bear witness to the word if you are going to go to war with it.

A Vision of Arrows in the Quiver

In 2015, my good friend Linda Milligan, codirector of the Key of David House of Prayer, approached me about joining forces with her on a prayer call to pray out the prophecies over our state, Florida. I immediately bore witness to this biblical strategy, and we wasted no time gathering intercessors and launching a weekly call.

Toward the end of our first prayer call I had a vision of an arrow being put into a quiver. The Lord told me that these prayer calls—these calls in which we pray out the many prophecies that have been declared over our state in the decades past—are an arrow in our quiver.

In other words the prayer call is a new weapon for the season in which we find ourselves. This arrow in the quiver is a prophetic strategy that can be used to hit our prayer target. Our prayer target is awakening. We want to see Florida, widely known in the nation as the Forerunner State or the First Fruits State, fulfill its destiny.

That said, we recognize that these calls are not the end-all. They are but one arrow in the quiver—one strategy that the Lord has given us. But I believe the prayer call is a strategy that will lead to a tipping point to bring revivals in cities from the Panhandle all the way down to Key West. And I believe it is a prophetic strategy that intercessors in other states can use to see their destinies come to pass.

God's hand is on our hands

After the vision, the Holy Spirit took me to 2 Kings 13. Here we find the prophet Elisha sick with the illness from which he would eventually die. King Joash of Israel came down to meet him, and the prophet gave him a prophetic strategy:

> Elisha said to him, "Take a bow and arrows. So he took a bow and arrows. Then he said to the king of Israel, "Draw the bow." So he drew it. Elisha put his hands on the king's hands.
>
> Then he said, "Open the east window." So he opened it. Then Elisha said, "Shoot." So he shot. Then he said, "The arrow of the deliverance of the LORD, and the arrow of deliverance from Aram; for you must strike Aram in Aphek until you have destroyed them."
>
> —2 KINGS 13:15–17

When I read this scripture, the Holy Spirit impressed on me that as we pray out the prophecies, His hands will literally be upon our hands. The Holy Spirit will labor with us to release the prayers. The angels of God will hearken to the voice of God's prophetic words to wage war in the heavenlies against the principalities and powers that are delaying the prophetic promises (Ps. 103:20). This is powerful!

Strike the ground!

That wasn't the end of Elisha's instructions to King Joash, and it is not the end of this prophetic strategy either. Let's review Elisha's next instruction to the king:

> Then he said, "Take the arrows." So he took them. Then he said to the king of Israel, "Strike the ground." So he struck it three times and stood there. Then the man of God was angry with him and said, "You should have struck it five or six times. Then you would have stricken Aram until you had finished them. Now you will strike Aram just three times."
>
> —2 Kings 13:18–19

We are praying out the prophecies over our state, but this is not a one-time prayer call. This is a strategy that brings victory through consistency. On the call I declared that we would not stop striking the ground but we would strike and strike and strike and strike and strike—and keep on striking until we see God's will manifest over our cities and in this state.

I believe this is a strategy for the body of Christ in this hour. Intercessors, I urge you to pray into this and see if God would have you implement a similar prayer call in your state and corporate prayer meetings in your city. General cries of repentance and prayers for awakening are important, but God is breathing on this strategy to pray out the prophetic words over your cities, regions, and states.

This Is a Fight We're In

First Timothy 1:18 exhorts us to be "inspired and aided" by the prophetic words that "you may wage the good warfare" (AMPC). The New Living Translation tells us that the prophetic words "help you fight well in the Lord's battles." And *The Message* tells us the prophecies should make you "fearless in your struggle, keeping a firm grip on your faith and on yourself. After all, this is a fight we're in."

Indeed, this is a fight we're in—it is a good fight of faith against unseen enemies. "For our fight is not against flesh and blood, but against principalities, against powers, against the rulers of the darkness of this world, and against spiritual forces of evil in the heavenly places" (Eph. 6:12). Thankfully, the unseen God—and unseen angels—are on our side. The angels are an important part of this spiritual warfare equation.

Think of Daniel. He had a prophetic vision that took him into prayer and fasting for three whole weeks. That prophetic vision, along with prayer and fasting, was followed by an angelic encounter from which we can learn plenty. The angel spoke to Daniel:

> For from the first day that you set your heart to understand this and to humble yourself before your God, your words were heard, and I have come because of your words. But the prince of the kingdom of Persia withstood me for twenty-one days. So Michael, one of the chief princes, came to help me, for I had been left there with the kings of Persia.
>
> —Daniel 10:12–13

Unleashing a Heavenly Host

Angels are still warring in the heavenlies. God can dispatch them—Jesus said He could pray and God would send twelve legions (that's 72,000 angels) to rescue Him (Matt. 26:47–54). God told Moses He would send an angel before him to drive the enemies out of the land (Exod. 33:2). But angels also obey the voice of His word (Ps. 103:20). That includes the written Word and true prophetic words.

So we see that waging warfare with the proven prophetic words we have received is scriptural—and that angels hearken unto the voice of His word. The question is, how do we wield this weapon? We pray it through. We decree it. We declare it. We meditate on it so that it gets down so deep in our spirit that when we pray it, decree it, and declare it, it carries authority that comes through faith.

We are fighting a good fight of faith more than we are fighting any enemy. The enemy is real, but the fight is often the fight to believe God's Word is true in the face of contrary circumstances. Scripture is the final authority and it is our sword, but tested prophetic words are like arrows in our quiver that we can shoot into the spirit realm to hit the target of God's revealed will. It is time to go back and review some of your prophetic words and rise up against the enemies that are standing in the way of your destiny.

Digging Out Your Prophetic Words

When it comes to personal prophecy, you can prepare for battle by digging up those old prophetic words that haven't come to pass. Maybe you put it on the shelf because it didn't make any sense to your natural mind at the time, but the Holy Spirit is now highlighting it to you in this season. Perhaps the prophetic promise was so exceedingly, abundantly above all you could ask or think that you dismissed it without even praying it through.

But sometimes even the wildest prophecies can be God's truth. So, again, it may be time to dig some of those old prophetic words out of a drawer. And if you aren't keeping a record of your prophetic words, you should start. When you receive a personal prophecy from a prophet—or when the Lord speaks to your heart or gives you a prophetic dream or vision—you should record it.

Some prophecies are like a heads up from God. It may not make any sense at the time, but later, when certain events begin to unfold in your life, that prophecy can serve as a confirmation that you are smack-dab in the middle of God's will. When you first hear the prophecy, you may not be in a place to receive it or comprehend it. But it may bring assurance and comfort later in life.

Either way, if you are going to pray out the prophecies in your life, you need record of them. So dig them out. Next, start meditating on the prophecy. Although prophecy is not on par with Scripture, prophecies that have been judged accurate can be acted upon. God is not done speaking to His people. Jesus said, "It is written, 'Man shall not live by bread alone, but by every word that proceeds out of the mouth of God'" (Matt. 4:4). Words are still proceeding out of God's mouth. They aren't Scripture, but they are still words from God that are alive.

God told Joshua that the Book of the Law must not depart from his mouth: "Meditate on it day and night so that you may act carefully according to all that is written in it. For then you will make your way successful, and you will be wise" (Josh. 1:8). Again, prophecy is not on par with Scripture, but if the prophetic word is in agreement with Scripture and judged to have proceeded out of God's mouth—not a human spirit or an evil spirit—then you can use it as a weapon of warfare.

Remember, "The weapons of our warfare are not carnal, but mighty through God to the pulling down of strongholds" (2 Cor. 10:4). Prophetic words that are not carnal—not soulish and certainly not demonic—are mighty weapons that can pull down strongholds that are holding back the promises of God.

Along with meditating on the prophetic word—rolling it over in your mind—you can confess the prophecies. The Bible says "faith comes by hearing, and hearing by the word of God" (Rom. 10:17). Your confession—saying the same thing Jesus says about you—is part of waging war with the prophetic words. You are essentially coming into agreement with the prophecy and demonstrating your faith by the act of confession.

Bible teacher Joyce Meyer sometimes says, "Words are containers of power."[4] Indeed, the power of death and life are in the tongue (Prov. 18:21). When you confess the prophecy out of your mouth, you are releasing the power it contains to bring itself to pass and simultaneously building your faith for the next phase of the journey: decreeing, declaring, and all-out warring with the prophecy.

How do you war with a prophetic word? How do you step into that 1 Timothy 1:18 reality? Practically speaking, you pray through it line by line. Suppose you get a prophetic word that says this: "I am preparing you to be a vessel of change in your city. I am calling you to make an impact in your region. I am equipping you to press into new levels of My glory so that you can carry My presence into dark territories."

After you meditate on it and confess it out of your mouth, you would pray it out in a manner such as this: "I thank You, Lord, that You are preparing me to be a vessel of change in my city. I thank You for the opportunity to serve You in this way, and I yield to Your preparation. Lord, show me what You need me to do to cooperate with You, to prepare myself for this mission, and give me the grace to do it. Thank You for this calling to make an impact on my region. Lord, please give me strategies and tactics and send laborers to work alongside me. Thank

You for equipping me to press into new levels of Your glory. Show me Your glory. Show me how to carry Your presence into dark territories for Your glory. Show me what steps to take. Lead me and guide me by Your Spirit, in the name of Jesus."

Wrestling With God—and Your Flesh

If you are wrestling, it may not be with principalities and powers—sometimes you wrestle with your flesh. Sometimes you wrestle with God because you don't want to let go of habits, thought patterns, or other ties that bind. Sometimes meditating, confessing, declaring, decreeing, and warring are not enough if your flesh won't get out of the way. You may have done everything you know to do, but the prophetic still has not come to pass.

In fact, it may even look like the exact opposite is happening in your life. It may look like the enemy has already robbed your prophecy. It may seem like the prophetic word will never come to pass. Now is your moment of decision. Will you give up on that tried-and-tested prophetic word that you know that you know that you know is from God? Or will you go back to the author of that prophecy—Jesus—and remind Him of the prophetic word and let Him win the wrestling match against your flesh?

Jacob got a prophetic word from God while he was fleeing his angry brother, Esau, whom he cheated out of his birthright. Imagine the scene: Jacob was traveling alone from Beersheba toward Haran. When the sun started setting, he decided to rest. He used a rock for a pillow and had prophetic dreams of "a ladder set up on the earth with the top of it reaching to heaven. The angels of God were ascending and descending on it" (Gen. 28:12). Next came a prophecy that was exceedingly abundantly above all he could ask or think:

> The LORD stood above it and said, "I am the LORD God of Abraham your father and the God of Isaac. The land on which you lie, to you will I give it and to your descendants. Your descendants will be like the dust of the earth, and you will spread abroad to the west and to the east and to the north and to the south, and in you and in your descendants all the families of the earth will be blessed. Remember, I am with you, and I will protect you wherever you go, and I will bring you back to this land. For I will not leave you until I have done what I promised you."
>
> —GENESIS 28:13–15

Jacob believed the prophetic word, set up a pillar to God, poured oil upon it, and made a vow to give a tenth to God if He kept him safe during his journey, gave him food and clothing, and allowed him to reach his father's house in peace. Of course, God kept up His part of the covenant. Despite being cheated by his uncle Laban for more than a decade, Jacob prospered wildly in every respect in Haran. He had exceedingly abundant children and livestock, and favor with God.

Finally fed up with Laban's dishonesty, Jacob decided to return to his country. Laban pursued him, and Jacob boldly confronted his uncle. But when Jacob learned that Esau was coming out to meet him, fear struck his heart. Jacob did what we need to do when it looks like our prophetic word can't possibly come to pass—when it looks like the devil is devouring our prophetic dreams. When the enemy comes in with fear that what God said will never happen, we need to take the prophetic word back to its author in prayer.

> And Jacob said, "O God of my father Abraham and God of my father Isaac, the LORD who said to me, 'Return to your country and to your relatives, and I will prosper you,' I am not worthy of all the lovingkindness and of

> all the faithfulness which You have shown to Your servant. For with my staff I crossed over this Jordan, and now I have become two encampments. Deliver me, I pray, from the hand of my brother, from the hand of Esau. For I fear him, that he will come and attack me and the mothers with the children. You said, 'I will surely prosper you and make your descendants as the sand of the sea, which is too many to be counted.'"
>
> —Genesis 32:9–12

But Jacob didn't stop there. Jacob wrestled with God over the issue until the break of day. You will recall the determined words of Jacob's mouth: "I will not let You go, unless You bless me" (Gen. 32:26). Jacob got his blessing, but he walked away with a limp. He let God win the wrestling match.

Of course, God always intended to keep His prophetic word to Jacob. There was never a question in God's mind whether or not He would watch over His word to perform it (Jer. 1:12). And the same holds true for you. Although some prophecies are conditional, some are set in stone—no man on earth or devil in hell can stop what God has planned. But we can stop it with our doubt, unbelief, fearful mind-set, complacency, and apathy—or carnality. Sometimes it is really a war on our flesh we need to wage.

So if you have been waiting for months, years, or decades for a prophecy to come to pass—and when you are afraid people and circumstances are going to kill your promise—do what Jacob did. Pray. Remind God of His prophetic word. Wrestle with God in prayer until you have the faith to get up and run toward His perfect will despite what things look like, even if you have to run with a limp because you have died to another layer of yourself.

CHAPTER 10

PRESSING INTO THRONE ROOM PRAISE AND WORSHIP

JAY AND HIS men were surrounded on all sides by enemy forces. There was no escaping—and they were far outnumbered. A sea of well-armed, well-trained, well-organized troops was fast approaching. And Jay wasn't up against just one enemy. He was up against three fierce armies intent on utterly annihilating him and everyone with him.

Jay's men were looking to him for leadership, and he had no answers. His adrenaline was racing through his body on overdrive. He started sweating and shaking. He got a sick feeling in his stomach as fear started taking over. No matter where he looked, there was no way of escape. He was not equipped to handle an onslaught from three enemy forces at once. His men would have fled, but there was nowhere to turn. He was running out of time before the enemy fired the first shot.

That's when Jay got down on his knees and prayed to God. He called everyone—soldiers and civilians alike—to fast and pray and seek the Lord. Jay knew that his only hope was in the God who is mighty to save. He stood before the people and cried out to God, reminding Him of His covenant as the whole nation—including women, children, and babies—looked on.

Suddenly, a prophet arose from the group with a prophetic warfare strategy straight from the throne that promised victory over all Jay's enemies. When they followed that prophetic warfare strategy line upon line, their enemies—all of them—fell, and God was the hero. Of course, that Jay I am talking about is none other than King Jehoshaphat. Let's look at this dramatic account in Scripture.

Second Chronicles 20 opens with a frightening scene. The Moabites, Ammonites, and Meunites decided to engage in battle with Jehoshaphat. Word came to the king that "a large multitude is coming against you from across the Dead Sea from Edom" (2 Chron. 20:2). The Bible says that Jehoshaphat was fearful and set himself to seek the Lord, and called a fast throughout all Judah. Understanding the urgency of the matter, the Bible says, "Judah was assembled to seek the LORD, even from all the cities of Judah, they came to obtain aid from the LORD" (2 Chron. 20:4).

Reminding God of His Covenant

Facing massive pressure from a fast-approaching army, Jehoshaphat didn't moan, groan, grumble, and complain about the situation he found himself in. He didn't sit and feel sorry for himself and feed his flesh with dainty foods. He didn't jump in bed, pull the covers over his head, and hope the devil would go away. (That is what some spiritual warriors do when the heat of the battle gets too hot for their soul.)

No, Jehoshaphat first reminded God of His covenant. That is a good place to start in spiritual battle. Really, you aren't reminding God so much as you are reminding yourself of that covenant. That blood covenant gives you forgiveness of sins. It is a good idea to repent of any sins of commission or omission—to examine your heart—when you are facing fierce battles. Repent before you enter the battlefield.

The covenant gives you authority to use the name above all names, the name at which every knee must bow (Phil. 2:10). That covenant promises that "no weapon that is formed against you shall prosper" (Isa. 54:17). That covenant promises that "greater is He who is in you than he who is in the world" (1 John 4:4, NASB). That covenant promises that God always leads you into triumph in Christ (2 Cor. 2:14). Are you getting the picture? Jehoshaphat didn't even have all of those promises, but he knew the power that was in the covenant he did have with God. Let's listen to Jehoshaphat's prayer in 2 Chronicles 20:6–12:

> O LORD God of our fathers, are You not God in the heavens? And do You not rule over all the kingdoms of the nations? In Your hand are strength and might, and there is no one who can oppose You. Did You not, our God, drive out those who lived in this land before Your people Israel, and You gave it perpetually to the descendants of Abraham, who was in covenant love with You. And they have dwelled in it and have built in it for You a sanctuary for Your name saying, "If disaster comes upon us, the sword, or judgment, or pestilence, or famine, then we will stand before this temple and before You because Your name is in this temple. And we will cry out to You in our distress, and You will hear and deliver."
>
> Now here are the sons of Ammon and Moab and Mount Seir, whom You did not let Israel invade when they came out of the land of Egypt, when they turned away from them and did not destroy them. See how they are rewarding us by coming to drive us out of Your possession, which You have given us to inherit. O our God, will You not render judgment on them? For we have not strength enough to stand before this great army that is coming against us. And we do not know what we should do, but our eyes are on You.

That is a pretty bold prayer! See the pattern. Jehoshaphat first honored God and His power among the nations. He acknowledged that Israel's success against its enemies was by the Father's hand. He reminded Him of the Abrahamic covenant and that His name was on the temple. And here's the bold part: Jehoshaphat reminded God that He did not allow Israel to conquer the enemies that were now invading Judah. Jehoshaphat asked Jehovah to pay close attention to how the Moabites, Ammonites, and Meunites were repaying His people for such mercy and called for judgment against the enemy. Then, the king kept his eyes on the King—and the King responded.

God's Prophetic Warfare Strategy Explained

I imagine there was a long pause as Jehoshaphat ended his prayer. It was a desperate prayer. It was a bold prayer. It was a specific prayer. It was an anointed prayer—and God bowed down His ear to hear. Imagine the scene. The Bible says all of Judah was standing before the Lord, even infants, wives, and children. Suddenly the Holy Ghost came on Jahaziel, a Levite, and he began to prophesy the first stage of the prophetic warfare strategy in 2 Chronicles 20:15–17:

> And he said, "Pay attention all Judah, and those dwelling in Jerusalem, and King Jehoshaphat: Thus says the Lord to you, 'Do not fear, nor be dismayed because of this great army, for the battle is not yours, but God's. Tomorrow, go down against them. They will travel up by the Ascent of Ziz. You will find them at the back of the valley, before the Wilderness of Jeruel. It will not be necessary for you to fight in this conflict. Take your positions, stand, and observe the deliverance of the Lord for you, O Judah and Jerusalem.' Do not fear or be filled with terror. Tomorrow, go out before them, and the Lord will be with you."

Again, this was stage one of the prophetic warfare strategy. It is important to understand that the Holy Spirit will not always reveal to you the entire plan up front. The just shall live—and war—by faith. We walk by faith and not by sight. Spiritual warfare requires faith in the warrior who has armed you for victorious battle. The Holy Spirit will lead you and guide you into the truth that you need to know when you need to know it.

This prophetic word was enough for Jehoshaphat. He no longer feared:

> Then Jehoshaphat bowed his face to the ground, and all Judah and those dwelling in Jerusalem fell before the LORD to worship Him. And the Levites from the descendants of the Kohathites and Korahites rose up to praise the LORD God of Israel with a very loud voice.
>
> —2 CHRONICLES 20:18–19

The next morning they went out and Jehoshaphat offered instructions for war. These instructions were not part of the prophecy, but I believe he was Spirit-led in these words and actions:

> Jehoshaphat stood and said, "Listen to me, Judah and those dwelling in Jerusalem. Believe in the LORD your God, and you will be supported. Believe His prophets, and you will succeed." And he consulted with the people and then appointed singers for the LORD and those praising Him in holy attire as they went before those equipped for battle saying, "Praise the LORD, for His mercy endures forever."
>
> —2 CHRONICLES 20:20–21

This was the second part of the prophetic warfare strategy. The prophecy didn't instruct Jehoshaphat to appoint singers for the Lord to go before the army. But the prophecy did make it clear that the soldiers would not have to fight. What is the natural thing to do when you already have the victory? What is the right response when the Lord has promised to deliver your enemy into your hand? Certainly, praise and worship! This is a powerful precept. When you come under heavy enemy fire, what would happen if you began to praise and worship God like you already had the victory—because you do—instead of moaning, groaning, grumbling, complaining, feeding your flesh, looking for a way of natural escape, and so on?

Believing the Prophets Unto Victory

Jehoshaphat said something interesting after Jahaziel prophesied. He said, "Believe His prophets, and you will succeed" (2 Chron. 20:20). That scripture has been twisted at times by controlling prophets who think you must obey their every command or you will fall under a curse. But there is a fundamental truth in what Jehoshaphat said.

When a true prophet offers a true prophetic word about a warfare strategy—or anything else—you will succeed when you walk it out. Of course, you don't have to be a prophet to get a prophetic warfare strategy. If you are filled with the Holy Spirit, you can hear His voice instruct you in battle. Let's look at how this prophetic warfare strategy played out in 2 Chronicles 20:22–23:

> When they began singing and praising, the Lord set ambushes against Ammon, Moab, and Mount Seir, who had come against Judah; so they were defeated. Then the Ammonites and Moabites stood up against those dwelling from Mount Seir to destroy and finish them. Then when they made an end of the inhabitants of Seir, each man attacked his companion to destroy each other.

Did you catch that? It was just as the prophetic word said. Judah did not have to lift a finger to fight. The battle truly was the Lord's. When we engage in praise and worship when all hell is breaking loose against us, it releases confusion into the enemy's camp. Paul understood this all too well. That is why he told the church at Philippi, "Do not be frightened by your adversaries. This is a sign to them of their destruction, but of your salvation, and this from God" (Phil. 1:28).

It has been said that dogs can tell if you are scared. Well, so can devils—and devils feed off your fear. When you give yourself over to fear, worry, guilt, or anything contrary to the love of God, you are inviting the enemy to bring confusion to your mind. By contrast, your praise and worship ushers you into the peace of God and literally causes confusion in the enemy's camp. Even if you feel afraid, don't speak it and don't let fear lead you. Instead, praise and worship and watch God turn the situation around. It may not happen immediately, but it will happen.

Inspired by the Holy Spirit, Paul said your salvation comes from God. The word *salvation* comes from the Greek word *soteria*, which implies "deliverance, preservation, safety, salvation."[1]

Something else happens when we execute the prophetic warfare strategy: we get the spoils of war. When Judah came to the watchtower of the wilderness, they turned toward the army and saw dead bodies everywhere. The enemies were utterly destroyed. Judgment fell on the enemy's camp. The Bible says no one was spared. Read this account in 2 Chronicles 20:25–26:

> Then Jehoshaphat and his people came to gather their plunder, and they found among them an abundance of riches with the corpses, and precious jewelry, which they took for themselves, more than they could carry. They

> were gathering the plunder for three days because there was so much to carry. On the fourth day they gathered at the Valley of Berakah, because there they blessed the LORD. For this reason people have called the name of this place the Valley of Berakah until this day.

That Hebrew word *Berakah* means "blessing."[2] Jehoshaphat went from fear to blessings when he followed the prophetic warfare strategy. It is important to note that the king did not act in presumption. Many spiritual warriors fall into this trap of adding to or taking away from God's instruction and end up losing the battle and blaming God—or the prophetic person that delivered the warfare strategy. It is vital to follow God's blueprint for battle and to thank Him for the victory. Judah did just that. We see how the story ends in 2 Chronicles 20:27–30:

> Then they all returned, every man from Judah and Jerusalem, with Jehoshaphat as their head, to Jerusalem with joy because the LORD made them rejoice because of the death of their enemies. So they entered Jerusalem with harps, lyres, and trumpets to the house of the LORD.
>
> And it happened that the terror of God was on all the kingdoms of the lands who heard that the LORD had fought against the enemies of Israel. So the kingdom of Jehoshaphat was quiet, because his God gave him rest on all sides.

Amen!

Do Not Remain Silent

You have probably read the story of Willie Myrick, the nine-year-old boy who didn't have a lot of discernment but packed a powerful punch with praise.

As the story goes, a kidnapper in Atlanta wooed little Willie with cash. When the boy walked close enough to the criminal's car, the man abducted him.[3] Like I said, the little boy may not have discerned the kidnapper's evil motives, but he certainly knew where to turn when he realized he'd been taken captive in a criminal's car.

Willie starting singing Grammy Award–winning gospel singer Hezekiah Walker's song, "Every Praise."[4] Willie didn't just sing high praise to God once. No, the little boy did it over and over and over and over again—for three hours. He later told news reporters that the kidnapper went into a cursing fit and eventually stopped the car and tossed him out (thankfully, no worse for the wear).[5]

"He opened the door and threw me out," Willie told Atlanta television station WXIA-TV. "He told me not to tell anyone."[6]

Of course, the young boy refused to remain silent in the car or after he got out. Willie's testimony glorified God. His story went viral on YouTube, demonstrating to the masses the power of praise. Hezekiah Walker was so touched by the story that he took time to meet with little Willie.[7]

Maybe Willie had read about Paul and Silas in the Book of Acts. Paul cast a devil out of a girl with divination, and when her masters saw that they could no longer use her perverted spiritual gifts to make money, they got angry and turned the apostles over to the authorities. The magistrates tore off the apostles' clothes and beat them with rods before throwing them into the inner prison with stocks on their feet. Look what happened next in Acts 16:25–28:

> At midnight Paul and Silas were praying and singing hymns to God, and the prisoners were listening to them. Suddenly there was a great earthquake, so that the foundations of the prison were shaken. And immediately all the doors were opened and everyone's shackles were

> loosened. When the jailer awoke and saw the prison doors open, he drew his sword and would have killed himself, supposing that the prisoners had escaped. But Paul shouted, "Do not harm yourself, for we are all here."

Get this. When it looked like all was lost—at the midnight hour—Paul and Silas were not moaning, groaning, grumbling, complaining, feeding their flesh, or planning a jailbreak. They were praying and singing hymns to God. That was their prophetic warfare strategy. They didn't try to manipulate the guards to let them go. They didn't get mad at God for allowing them to be taken captive. The Bible doesn't offer the content of their prayers, but I believe they prayed for God to deliver them and then praised Him in advance.

In that moment, when they least expected it, God moved and there was an earthquake—and not just any earthquake: a great earthquake! The Greek word for *earthquake* is *seismos*, which means "a shaking, a commotion; a tempest; an earthquake."[8] Paul and Silas touched the heart of God in heaven, and He literally moved the earth in response. God delivered them, and their freedom served as a witness to the many in that jail cell who were listening to them praise their God. God was glorified.

Can you imagine singing hymns to God while in a dungeon, likely waiting to be executed? How about singing a Hezekiah Walker song in a car with a kidnapper? In both instances the captives were waging spiritual warfare against the real enemy—the spirits that motivated the attack against them.

Spiritual Warfare With Praise and Worship

Praise and worship is a powerful weapon in our spiritual warfare arsenal. Praise brought down the walls at Jericho (Josh. 6). And let's not forget David's anointed music that delivered Saul from distressing spirits (1 Sam. 16:14–17, 23). Indeed, the Bible speaks of "songs of deliverance" in Psalm 32:7 (KJV).

We read these scriptures, yet how many of us actually sing praise and worship to God in the midst of our battles? How many of us do what Paul and Silas did and sing hymns to God when the enemy has us bound up? How many do what Willie did and refuse to stop singing praises to our God when the enemy is threatening us?

God is always with you, but if you want to unleash more power in spiritual warfare, try more praise and worship and less screaming at the devil. I assure you, I've tried both, and praise and worship is a sharper weapon than the loudest, boldest voice binding the devil. I am not opposed to getting loud, mind you. But greater volume does not always ensure a greater (or faster) victory.

What do we sing? We sing His praises. We sing about who He is. We sing about His beauty. We sing about His mercy. We sing about His justice. We sing about His love in songs such as "I Could Sing of Your Love Forever," a song originally written by Martin Smith of the British Christian rock band Delirious?.

What do we sing? We sing about His delivering power. We sing about His goodness. We sing about His faithfulness. God inhabits the praises of His people (Ps. 22:3). "Let us sing to the LORD...shout joyfully to the Rock of our salvation...come before His presence with thanksgiving...shout joyfully to Him with psalms" (Ps. 95:1–2, NKJV). Let us "worship the LORD in the splendor of holiness" (Ps. 29:2, ESV). Exalt the Lord and worship at His footstool (Ps. 99:5).

What do we sing? We can literally sing God's Word. When we sing God's Word—about provision, healing, salvation for our families, or anything else—we bring light into our hearts and into the atmosphere around us. Satan can't stand the light. Worshipping God is resisting the temptation to look at the enemy. Praising Him keeps our focus on the Prince of Peace rather than the prince of the power of the air.

In the song of Moses in Exodus 15:2–3, the children of Israel sang a song to the Lord that went something like this:

> The Lord is my strength and song, and He has become my salvation; He is my God, and I will praise Him; my father's God, and I will exalt Him. The Lord is a man of war; the Lord is His name.

Of course, that was after Israel had been delivered from Egypt. If you want to make the devil flee, praise God before you engage in battle. But don't forget to praise Him when the battle is won. David put it this way in Psalm 34:1–7:

> I will bless the Lord at all times; His praise will continually be in my mouth. My soul will make its boast in the Lord; the humble will hear of it and be glad. Oh, magnify the Lord with me, and let us exalt His name together. I sought the Lord, and He answered me, and delivered me from all my fears. They looked to Him and became radiant, and their faces are not ashamed. This poor man cried, and the Lord heard, and saved him out of all his troubles. The angel of the Lord camps around those who fear Him, and delivers them.

I could go on and on and on. I got the revelation of worship as spiritual warfare a long while ago. But little Willie's experience gave me a greater revelation—and a deeper confirmation—that we can ambush Satan with song. So the next time you find the enemy trying to take your thoughts captive—or wreak havoc on your natural circumstances—remember Paul, Silas, and Willie. And remember this:

> Praise the LORD! Praise God in His sanctuary; praise Him in the firmament of His power! Praise Him for His mighty acts; praise Him according to His excellent greatness! Praise Him with the sound of the trumpet; praise Him with the lyre and harp! Praise Him with the tambourine and dancing; praise Him with stringed instruments and flute! Praise Him with loud cymbals; praise Him with clashing cymbals! Let everything that has breath praise the LORD. Praise the LORD!
>
> —PSALM 150

Amen.

Chapter 11

TAPPING INTO THE PROPHETIC POWER OF TRAVAIL

When I'm not traveling from city to city ministering, I like to sit in my room on Saturday mornings with worship music on, my Bible at my left hand, and my journal at my right hand, and just soak. I like to meet with God in that secret place. I like to get refilled to overflowing with His Spirit. I like to hear His heart and His plans for the next leg of our journey together.

In fact, many of the devotions from my book *Mornings With the Holy Spirit: Listening Daily to the Still, Small Voice of God* came out of those times of worship and prayer in my secret place. It is a time of refreshing, a time of equipping, a time of intercession, a time when deep cries out to deep, a time of strategy, a time to receive whatever I need from the Lord. And He is always faithful to meet me there.

One morning after a long journey to the Navajo Nation in New Mexico, I was sitting in my usual spot—shut off from the world—just enjoying the presence of God. Suddenly I entered into travail unlike anything I had ever witnessed, experienced, or even read about before. Sure, I have seen an intercessor go into deep travail, bent halfway down with her hand over her belly as she raced to a back room to give herself over to the Holy Spirit in prayer. I have read plenty of books on intercession that talk about travail. And of course, I have read the Bible.

Before I continue with this story that taught me the prophetic power of travail, let's define *travail*. Paul discusses the spiritual practice in Romans 8:26–27:

> Likewise, the Spirit helps us in our weaknesses, for we do not know what to pray for as we ought, but the Spirit Himself intercedes for us with groanings too deep for words. He who searches the hearts knows what the mind of the Spirit is, because He intercedes for the saints according to the will of God.

These "groanings too deep for words" are one manifestation of travailing prayer. The Greek word for *groanings* in that scripture is *stenagmos*, which simply means "a groaning or a sigh."[1] *Merriam-Webster* defines *travail* as "a painful or difficult work or effort."[2] If you have ever entered into travail, you know that is true. In fact, it may be an understatement. *Webster's Revised Unabridged Dictionary* goes a little deeper, defining *travail* as "labor with pain; severe toil or exertion" and "to suffer the pangs of childbirth; to be in labor."[3] Again, if you have ever entered into travail, you can relate.

I had been in travail before that memorable day but never before like what I was about to experience. It started as I was praying fervently in the Spirit in my supernatural prayer language. The prayer took on a fevered pitch. I was praying hard and fast and fast and hard. Suddenly I entered into the groanings too deep for words—and it was loud. So loud, in fact, was this travail that there was a war going on in my mind.

See, I live in a condo on the beach, and the walls are thin. I figured my neighbors would be knocking on the door at any moment thinking I had gravely injured myself, or that the paddy wagon was surely on its way. My natural mind was trying to shut down the work of the Holy Spirit through me. Thankfully I was not ignorant to the practice of travail. I did not let my soul lead the way but allowed my spirit to take charge, yielding to the Holy Spirit. I didn't know it, but I was in for quite the wild ride.

I groaned and hollered in the Spirit so loud that my throat became sore. I was literally sweating. I thought the veins in my eyeballs would pop. My head started to hurt. The muscles in my abdomen were growing weary. Yet I continued to travail as Misty Edwards's high-tempo song was streaming over my computer in the background. I was pacing back and forth in my room, giving myself over to this experience, when suddenly I found myself on the ground. I was literally holding on to the bedposts, travailing as if my life depended on it.

Now, I have given birth to a baby. I won't go so far as to say that the pain was as severe, but I will testify that the experience was just as intense. After that episode—what I like to think of as a spiritual contraction—ended, I rose up and began speaking fervently in a tongue that I did not recognize. In other words, it was not my normal tongues for edification. It sounded like a known language, but I have no idea what language—or combination of languages—it was. I just knew in my spirit that I was at war with something I could not see and that God was battling through me unto victory. Again, there was a war in my mind, but I let my spirit lead.

After this spiritual contraction, for lack of better words, I went back into travail—deep travail. By this time I was wondering whether this birthing was ever going to end. Finally, it did. The "labor with pain" lasted between forty-five minutes and an hour. And when it ended, I was exhausted. Completely exhausted. I lay down in my bed as if I had just given birth to a newborn baby. I believe I did, in the spirit realm. I believe that I was birthing the next measure of my destiny and doing battle in the spirit against what was working to hinder my calling.

Of course, I didn't know that at the time. I had little (or I should say, no) discernment about what or whom I was praying and warring for. I just felt like I had been through a war. I lay in bed the rest of the day, discussed the experience with a few of my closest friends on the phone, and just rested in God. After that, I can tell you assuredly that my prayer life changed. I began praying with more authority and walking in more authority, including signs, wonders, and miracles.

There was no way I could have made that happen. I cannot repeat the process—but it is important to note that I could have stopped it. The Holy Spirit invites us into places with Him, but He doesn't force our hand. We don't have to go. Too many churches today are not only shutting out the intercessors but also quenching travail. We need to let God be God even if it makes religious people uncomfortable. And we need to teach about aspects of prayer like travail so that young believers understand these spiritual dynamics and are not afraid when they see or experience these types of things for themselves.

What It Really Means to Travail

When it comes to spiritual warfare—and intercession—many times we don't know how to pray as we ought. We sense spiritual oppression trying to discourage us, demons harassing people we love, or principalities settling over our cities like a dark rain cloud—but we don't always have revelation about the enemy we are fighting.

When that happens, I always do one thing: pray in the Spirit—and I don't stop praying in the Spirit until that oppression lifts or until I have a Spirit-inspired strategy to wrestle against what is wrestling against me. I wrestle from a place of victory, but I don't wrestle presumptuously. I need the Holy Spirit to show me how to pray—and sometimes that prayer includes travail, which is somewhat of a lost art in the body of Christ.

James Goll, cofounder of Encounters Network, defines *travail* like this:

> Travail is a form of intense intercession given by the Holy Spirit whereby an individual or group is gripped by a gestating promise that grips God's heart. The individual or group labors with Him in prayer so that the new life can come forth...Travail takes place after you have carried something in your heart for a period of time. It comes on you suddenly. It is preceded by nurturing the promise; later the strategic time comes to push that promise forth through the prayer canal. Finally you realize that the promise has been born, and you are greatly relieved when the delivery is over![4]

As I mentioned, we can't work up this type of prayer by our will. It is a spiritual response to a prayer burden. Travail has to be Spirit-led, or it is just soulish or fleshly. Nevertheless, travail is a genuine form of prayer that can break through when nothing else does. The word *travail* is found several times in the King James Version of the New Testament (and many more times in the Old). Travail births, but it also wars.

Barbara Yoder, founder of Shekinah Regional Apostolic Center, explains that, "Travail is a specific type of prayer which both births (Is. 66:7–9) as well as wars (Is. 42:12–14). When a person enters a time, period or season of travail (birthing and/or warring), they will experience it as a heaviness, weight, burden, deep penetrating concern or unease over a situation or condition that they cannot shake. Sometimes travail extends to weeks or months particularly when God burdens a person over a nation."[5]

When Jesus talked about the pregnant woman who had sorrow in travail (John 16:21), He was referring to *tikto*, which means "to bring forth, bear, produce (fruit from the seed); of a woman giving birth; of the earth bringing forth its fruits."[6] But when Paul was talking about interceding for the Thessalonians (1 Thess. 2:9), the Greek word for *travail* is *mochthos*, which means "a hard and difficult labor, toil, travail, hardship, distress."[7]

Hebrew words for *travail* include *yalad*, which also brings in the connotation of helping: "to cause or help to bring forth; to assist or tend as a midwife";[8] *tĕla'ah*, which implies seeking deliverance from toil, hardship, distress, and weariness;[9] *'inyan*, which refers to an occupation, task, or job;[10] *chalah*, which means to "be or become grieved, be or become sorry";[11] and *'amal*, which means "toil, trouble, labor."[12] (See Genesis 38:27; Exodus 18:8; Ecclesiastes 1:13; Isaiah 23:4; and Isaiah 53:11).

Cindy Jacobs, cofounder of Generals International, in her book *Possessing the Gates of the Enemy*, says, "There are times when we are called by God to pray strong prayers and help to birth the will of God into that area. Usually there is a sense of wonder after the prayer, and a sense that God has done something through it."[13]

Jacobs offers four points to help you recognize the work of the Holy Spirit:

> 1. Travail is given by God and is not something we can make happen…
>
> 2. Travail sometimes comes as a result of praying in an area that others have prayed about before you. God then chooses you to be one of the last pray-ers before the matter is accomplished. You are the one who gives birth to the answer.

3. Those with the gift of intercession will often pray more travailing prayers than those who are not as open to the Lord's using them in this manner...

4. The travail may be short or extended. Some prayers will be accomplished quickly, and some will be like labor pangs at different times until the birth of the answer comes.[14]

The Power of Travail in Warfare

The power of travail in warfare is, well, powerful. As Yoder mentioned, we find the warring type of travail in Isaiah 42. Let's look at a few verses and notice how the travail started in the midst of worship, just like in the experience I shared earlier. This passage is from Isaiah 42:10–17:

> Sing to the Lord a new song, and His praise from the ends of the earth, you who go down to the sea, and all that is in it, the coastlands, and the inhabitants. Let the wilderness and the cities lift up their voices, the villages that Kedar inhabits. Let the inhabitants of Sela sing, let them shout from the top of the mountains. Let them give glory to the Lord, and declare His praise in the islands. The Lord shall go forth like a mighty man; He shall stir up zeal like a man of war. He shall cry out, yes, raise a war cry; He shall prevail against His enemies.
>
> I have for a long time held My peace; I have been still and refrained Myself. Now I will cry like a travailing woman; I will destroy and devour at once. I will lay waste mountains and hills and dry up all their vegetation, and I will make the rivers islands, and I will dry up the pools. I will bring the blind by a way that they did not know; I will lead them in paths that they have not known. I will make darkness light before them and

> crooked things straight. These things I will do for them and not forsake them. They shall be turned back, they shall be greatly ashamed, who trust in graven images, who say to the molded images, "You are our gods."

What happens when the Lord travails is pretty intense. When it comes to prophetic warfare strategies, we want to let the Holy Spirit travail with us and scatter our enemies. In fact, we may even see enemies scattered that we didn't know we were facing. Just like we pray in the Spirit—and our spirit prays with the Holy Spirit—we can travail by the Spirit. We are doing the travailing, but the Holy Spirit is coming alongside us to travail with us.

The word *cry* in verse 13 is the Hebrew word *ruwa`*, which means "to shout a war-cry or alarm of battle; to sound a signal for war or march; to shout in triumph (over enemies); to shout in applause; to shout (with religious impulse); to cry out in distress; to utter a shout; to shout in triumph; to shout for joy."[15] A second category of definition for *cry* in these verses is "destroyed."[16] The word *cry* in verse 14 comes from the Hebrew word *pa'ah*, which means "to groan, cry out, scream."[17] This is the travailing aspect of that passage. You can be assured that when the Holy Spirit leads you into a war cry followed by travail, the assignment of the enemy will be completely destroyed.

Travail That Brings Deliverance

Most of the time travailing prayer is a birthing prayer—it births something you have been carrying in your heart that God wants to deliver. But it can also be a deliverance prayer, which is an aspect of spiritual warfare. In this verse, *travail* is used in the context of deliverance:

> And Moses told his father in law all that the Lord had done unto Pharaoh and to the Egyptians for Israel's sake,

> and all the travail that had come upon them by the way, and how the LORD delivered them.
>
> —EXODUS 18:8, KJV

Sometimes, when the enemy gets an advantage over us (2 Cor. 2:11), another person, or even a region, the Spirit of God will lead you into travailing prayer. You serve as a midwife and toil in prayer to help bring forth God's purposes—to birth His will in the earth—which may also mean deliverance from the kingdom of darkness.

As James Goll explains, "The prayer of travail is God desiring to create an 'opening' to bring forth a measure of life or growth. If the 'opening' was already in place, there would not be the need for travail." Goll continued, "Just as the 'opening' of the natural womb is enlarged to bring forth the baby, so travail creates an 'opening' or 'way,' whereas before the opening or way was closed. With travail, there is always a way opened for life, newness, change, or growth."[18]

Many times before travailing prayer comes upon you, you will feel grieved, heavy, or otherwise burdened. Less experienced intercessors may believe they are under spiritual attack—and they may be—but it is often the Holy Spirit moving on a person's spirit to engage in travail with Him. Notice I say "with Him." Again, you cannot stir up travail in your soul or your flesh. It is Spirit-inspired. I just can't stress that too much. The important thing to know is that when you sense this coming on you, you need to yield to the Holy Spirit to birth His purposes—or to deliver or wage war.

Travail is not prayer led by emotions, though you may appear emotional as you enter travail with weeping and wailing and groaning like a woman birthing a child. Because of its intensity, some churches have relegated intercession to a back room and essentially thrown the baby out with the breakthrough bathwater. But it is vital that we cooperate with the Holy Spirit when He wants to use us as midwives to birth or deliver, even if we have to excuse ourselves from the prayer meeting to avoid confusing those who are not familiar with this type of intercession.

"Many times travail can be so strong that it seems to overwhelm the intercessor," says Cindy Jacobs. "Those around need to intercede for the one in travail if this happens in a group situation. We need to help bear the burden in prayer...We also need to watch after that one by binding the enemy from entering into the travail. One word of caution. The Holy Spirit will rule over our emotions in a time of travail. We must be sure that we don't let our emotions run wild. Intercessors need to walk in the fruit of self-control."[19]

Letting the Holy Spirit Pray Through You

With all this in mind let's look at Romans 8 again:

> We know that the whole creation groans and travails in pain together until now. Not only that, but we also, who have the first fruits of the Spirit, groan within ourselves while eagerly waiting for adoption, the redemption of our bodies. For we are saved through hope, but hope that is seen is not hope, for why does a man still hope for what he sees? But if we hope for what we do not see, we wait for it with patience.
>
> Likewise, the Spirit helps us in our weaknesses, for we do not know what to pray for as we ought, but the Spirit Himself intercedes for us with groanings too deep for words. He who searches the hearts knows what the mind of the Spirit is, because He intercedes for the saints according to the will of God.
>
> —Romans 8:22–27

The will of God is to birth His purposes. The will of God is to deliver people from the bonds of Satan. The will of God is that we cooperate with His Holy Spirit, laboring in all manner of prayer to prevail in the wrestling match against principalities, powers, rulers of the darkness of this age, and spiritual hosts of wickedness in the heavenly places (Eph. 6:12). Sometimes all manner of prayer includes travail.

Chuck Pierce, founder of Glory of Zion International Ministries, explains that once this process begins and we identify what burden God wants us to pray over, we begin to agonize and feel the urgency of seeing the burden birthed:

> The burden becomes our own "baby" as God's heart for seeing that thing brought forth begins to press down on our spirits. With it comes an oppression, but it's not the oppression of the devil. If your assignment, for instance, is a travail to break an oppression over certain people on God's heart, you can actually begin to feel the oppression they are under. That is the time to travail until the oppression breaks—until, as in natural childbirth, the heavenly opening is large enough so that God's will can come forth on the earth.[20]

Chapter 12

PARTNERING WITH ANGELIC WARRIORS

I WILL NEVER FORGET my mountaintop experience in North Carolina. Well, I wasn't exactly on the top of the mountain, but I was far above the valley. My friend told me we were climbing up about a mile, but it was several miles before we settled into a secluded spot on the side of the Smoky Mountains.

I wasn't in great shape like I am today, so I was exhausted and starving with aching muscles I didn't even know I had. I felt like a weary warrior who had crucified every bit of flesh to conquer the mountain only to have the mountain conquer me. All I wanted to do was lie down, but we had to tie the food bag up on the pole, start a fire, and assemble the tent.

I'm a city girl, so I didn't know how to do any of those things, but I prayed fervently for my friend while she raced to get the job done before sundown. I figured it was the least she could do after telling me the climb was a mile when it was really five or six! What happened after sundown opened my eyes to a new level of the role of angels in spiritual warfare.

Sure, I understood that angels are "ministering spirits sent out to minister to those who will inherit salvation" (Heb. 1:14). I knew that the archangel Michael fought the prince of Persia (Dan. 10:13). I was aware of the promises of angelic protection in Psalm 91. But my eyes were opened that night when I heard a rustling outside the tent. I unzipped the door and was confronted with a demon darker than the night that caused me to leap backward in the tent with a screech.

I didn't know what it was, but I know it scared me good. Later, after discussing the event with one of my prophetic mentors, I discovered it was the spirit of fear coming to harass us. That didn't last long, though. My friend looked at me like I was nuts and decided to take a look out of the tent door for herself, despite my urgent warning (which may not have been distinguishable through my prayers in tongues).

When she opened the tent doors, I distinctly and repeatedly heard her utter three words I never would have expected: "Wow, wow, wow." She wasn't the least bit scared and waved me over to come take a look-see. I wasn't quite sure I could trust her, given that she'd measured five miles as one, but I mustered up all the courage I could manage and peeked out of the tent.

I saw nothing but the embers of a burning fire. She saw something else. She saw two angels standing at attention with swords drawn guarding the camp. She described them as beautiful, and she just gasped with awe. I squinted really hard but I still couldn't see anything but the glowing flames from the fire. I would have rather seen angels than a spirit of fear, but I was sure she saw the angels. This opened my eyes to how literal the Scripture is about angelic warriors.

Ranks of Spiritual Armies

Before we go deeper into partnering with angelic warriors, we need to understand the ranks of angels—both good and evil. We know Satan's kingdom is highly organized with a clear hierarchy. Likewise there are different types of angels with different functions in God's kingdom.

Let's look at the devil's kingdom first. Paul the apostle revealed this mystery in Ephesians 6:12: "For our fight is not against flesh and blood, but against principalities, against powers, against the rulers of the darkness of this world, and against spiritual forces of evil in the heavenly places."

Principalities are the highest level of demons. The word *principality* comes from the Greek word *arche*, which means "chief or ruler."[1] These are like the CEOs or five-star generals of the demonic realm, reporting directly to Satan himself. They set themselves over nations and territories.

Merriam-Webster defines *principality* as "the state, office, or authority of a prince" and "the territory or jurisdiction of a prince: the country that gives title to a prince."[2] Think of the prince of Persia, who is different than the king of Persia. The king was the natural ruler; the prince of Persia was a principality Michael fought (Dan. 10:13).

Powers are the next level. These are like the colonels in the army. The Greek word for *powers* in this verse is *exousia*, which means, "power, authority, weight, especially: moral authority, influence."[3] Jesus delegated His power to us and assured us we have authority over all the power of the enemy (Luke 10:19). The only authority a power has in your life is the power you give it through your thoughts, words, and actions.

The Greek word for *wickedness* in this verse is *ponéria*, which means "iniquity, wickedness, depravity, and malice."[4] *Malice* is defined as "desire to cause pain, injury, or distress to another" or "intent to commit an unlawful act or cause harm without legal justification or excuse," according to *Merriam-Webster*.[5] You may have had some run-ins with spiritual wickedness in heavenly places in your personal spiritual warfare.

The word *rulers* in Paul's phrase "rulers of the darkness of this world" comes from the Greek word *kosmokrator*. It means "lord of the world, prince of this age."[6] But what is this darkness over which they rule? Darkness in this verse comes from the Greek word *skotos*. It can mean "darkness, like night darkness." But in this context it means "of ignorance respecting divine things and human duties, and the accompanying ungodliness and immorality, together with their consequent misery in hell." It also means, "persons in whom darkness becomes visible and holds sway," according to *The KJV New Testament Greek Lexicon*.[7]

I believe this is where the hand-to-hand combat comes in. These are the demons that help enforce Satan's darkness that has "blinded the minds of those who do not believe, lest the light of the glorious gospel of Christ, who is the image of God, should shine on them" (2 Cor. 4:4). Evangelists often battle with the rulers of the darkness of this age when they set out to preach the gospel. This is why intercession is so important to backstop the work of an evangelist.

In the kingdom of God there are different types of angels with different roles. The seraphim are six-winged angels that stand in the presence of God and praise Him, crying, "Holy, holy, holy, is the Lord of Hosts; the whole earth is full of His glory" (Isa. 6:1–3). We would have a lot less trouble with the devil if we would enter into worship and praise His name when we sense enemy attacks rising against us. But that is the topic of another chapter in this book! We only see the seraphim in that portion of Isaiah.

We see cherubim much more often, from Genesis 3:24 to Exodus 25:18–22 to 1 Samuel 4:4 to 1 Kings 6:25 to Ezekiel's book, the Psalms, and beyond. God sent cherubim to guard the tree of life after the fall of man (Gen. 3:24); they are known as guards of the sacred things of God. They appeared over the ark of the covenant on the mercy seat and were embroidered on the temple veil (Exod. 25:22, 36:35). It is interesting to note that Lucifer was an anointed guardian cherub, not a warring angel, before his fall. You can read about that in Ezekiel 28:12–15:

> You had the seal of perfection, full of wisdom and perfect in beauty. You were in Eden, the garden of God; every precious stone was your covering: the sardius, topaz, and the diamond, the beryl, the onyx, and the jasper, the sapphire, the emerald, and the carbuncle, and gold. The workmanship of your settings and sockets was in you; on the day that you were created, they were prepared. You were the anointed cherub that covers, and I set you there; you were upon the holy mountain of God; you walked up and down in the midst of the stones of fire. You were perfect in your ways from the day that you were created, until iniquity was found in you.

Finally, there are the archangels. Gabriel and Michael are the two archangels named in the Bible, though there are likely others whose names we do not know. Gabriel appears as a messenger angel in Luke 1:11–20 and Luke 1:26–38, while Michael is definitely depicted as a warring angel in Daniel 10:13, Daniel 10:21, Daniel 12:1, and Revelation 12:7. These warring angels will be the ones we focus on in our study on waging prophetic warfare.

Michael the Warring Angel

Daniel had a prophetic vision that took him into prayer and fasting for three whole weeks. That prophetic vision, along with prayer and fasting, was followed by an angelic encounter from which we can learn plenty. The angel told Daniel that from the first day he started praying out that prophetic vision, God heard his words, and an angel came because of his words. Let's dig into this to see how angels war with us and for us.

> In the third year of Cyrus king of Persia a message was revealed to Daniel, whose name was called Belteshazzar, and the message was true and one of great conflict. And

he understood the message and had understanding of the vision.

In those days I, Daniel, was mourning three full weeks. I ate no tasty food, no meat or wine entered my mouth, nor did I anoint myself at all until three whole weeks were fulfilled.

On the twenty-fourth day of the first month, as I was by the side of the great river which is Tigris, I lifted up my eyes and looked and saw a certain man clothed in linen, whose loins were girded with the fine gold of Uphaz. His body also was like beryl, and his face had the appearance of lightning, and his eyes were like lamps of fire, and his arms and his feet were like the gleam of polished bronze, and the sound of his words like the sound of a tumult.

I, Daniel, alone saw the vision, while the men who were with me did not see the vision; but a great quaking fell upon them, so that they fled to hide themselves. Therefore I was left alone and saw this great vision, and there remained no strength in me, and my countenance grew deathly pale, and I retained no strength. Yet I heard the sound of his words; and while I heard the sound of his words, then I was in a deep sleep on my face with my face toward the ground.

But then a hand touched me, which set me on my knees and on the palms of my hands. He said to me, "O Daniel, a man greatly beloved, understand the words that I speak to you, and stand upright, for I have been sent to you now." And when he had spoken this word to me, I stood trembling.

Then he said to me, "Do not be afraid, Daniel. For from the first day that you set your heart to understand this and to humble yourself before your God, your words were heard, and I have come because of your words. But the prince of the kingdom of Persia withstood me for twenty-one days. So Michael, one of the chief princes,

> came to help me, for I had been left there with the kings of Persia. Now I have come to make you understand what shall befall your people in the latter days. For the vision is yet for many days."
>
> —Daniel 10:1–14

The angel that came to Daniel also explained:

> Then he said, "Do you understand why I have come to you? But now I shall return to fight against the prince of Persia, and when I have gone forth, then truly the prince of Greece will come. But I will show you what is inscribed in the Scripture of Truth. Yet there is no one who stands firmly with me against these forces, except Michael your prince."
>
> —Daniel 10:20–21

It is important for you to understand the principles in this passage as they relate to waging prophetic warfare. Daniel saw a prophetic vision that opened up the realities of the war in the heavenlies. When we pray—whether it's the prayer of faith, agreement, binding and loosing, or prophetic intercession—we don't always see an immediate result. Sometimes it's because we are out of God's timing. Sometimes it's because we are out of God's will. But sometimes it's because there is a demonic delay. That is when we need to partner with angelic warriors.

Partnering With Angelic Warriors

Even though Michael's war in the heavenlies was in the Old Testament, I assure you that angels are still warring in the heavenlies. If you need a New Testament example, I would point you to Michael's activities in Revelation 12:7–8: "Then war broke out in heaven. Michael and his angels fought against the dragon, and the dragon and his angels fought, but they did not prevail, nor was there a place for them in heaven any longer."

Indeed, angels are still warring in the heavenlies. God can dispatch them—Jesus said He could pray and God would send twelve legions (that's 72,000 angels) to rescue Him (Matt. 26:47–54). Psalm 103:20 explains that the angels do His commands and obey the voice of His Word. When we proclaim His Word, the angels listen and execute it. God's Word will not return to Him void, but it will accomplish that which He sends it to do. When you have a *rhema* word—a prophetically inspired unction to release the sword of the Spirit—the angels will listen and obey that word.

I never realized just how much angels are involved in warfare until I started to study the subject for this book. For example, we can claim and proclaim Exodus 23:20–23:

> Indeed, I am going to send an angel before you to guard you along the way and to bring you into the place which I have prepared. Be on guard before him and obey his voice. Do not provoke him, for he will not pardon your transgressions, for My name is in him. But if you diligently obey his voice and do all that I say, then I will be an enemy to your enemies and an adversary to your adversaries. For My angel will go before you and bring you to the Amorites, and the Hittites, and the Perizzites, and the Canaanites, the Hivites, and the Jebusites, and I will completely destroy them.

We also see that angels are integral in warfare in other passages. David's prayer was that his enemies would be as "chaff before the wind, and may the angel of the LORD cast them down" (Ps. 35:5). And 2 Kings 19:35–36 shows us that God answered those types of prayers:

> On that night the angel of the LORD went out and struck one hundred and eighty-five thousand in the camp of the Assyrians. When others woke up early in the morning, these were all dead bodies. So Sennacherib king of Assyria departed and stayed in Nineveh.

Of course, we're talking about spiritual warfare here. I am not advocating that you sic angels on people you don't like the way a homeowner would sic his pit bull on a burglar. That is not just foul; it is a wrong spirit, and God won't honor it. As a part of a Sermon on the Mount lifestyle, we are called to bless those who persecute us and despitefully use us. Even in the Old Testament, wisdom dictated, "If your enemy is hungry, give him bread to eat; and if he is thirsty, give him water to drink; for you will heap coals of fire upon his head, and the LORD will reward you" (Prov. 25:21–22).

Angels also go before us to guard us as we enter into battle. The psalmist said, "The chariots of God are twice ten thousand, even thousands of thousands; the LORD is among them, as in Sinai, in the holy place" (Ps. 68:17). The King James translation says "even thousands of angels." That verse reminds me of the account of Elisha's fearful servant in 2 Kings 6:12–17:

> Then one of his servants said, "No one, my lord, O king. Elisha, the prophet who is in Israel, tells the king of Israel the words that you speak in your bedroom."
>
> He said, "Go and see where he is, so that I may send for him and take him." And it was told to him, "He is in Dothan." So he sent horses, chariots, and a great army there. They came by night and surrounded the city.
>
> When a servant of the man of God rose early in the morning and went out, a force surrounded the city both with horses and chariots. And his servant said to him, "Alas, my master! What will we do?"

> And he said, "Do not be afraid, for there are more with us than with them."
>
> Then Elisha prayed, "LORD, open his eyes and let him see." So the LORD opened the eyes of the young man, and he saw that the mountain was full of horses and chariots of fire surrounding Elisha.

Angels Protect Us and Deliver Us in Warfare

Beyond warring for and with us, angels can also protect us and deliver us in the midst of spiritual warfare. Psalm 34:7 assures us, for example, that "The angel of the LORD camps around those who fear Him, and delivers them."

Psalm 91 is one passage of Scripture I claim over my life, my daughter, my family, my ministry, my finances, and everything else that pertains to me every morning. But these verses are particularly encouraging with regard to our discussion of the role of angels in waging prophetic warfare. Psalm 91:9–12 reads:

> Because you have made the LORD, who is my refuge, even the Most High, your dwelling, there shall be no evil befall you, neither shall any plague come near your tent; for He shall give His angels charge over you to guard you in all your ways. They shall bear you up in their hands, lest you strike your foot against a stone.

Sometimes angels protect us by warning us of danger that lies ahead. Such was the case with Joseph, the earthly father of Jesus, in Matthew 2:13:

> Now when they departed, the angel of the Lord appeared to Joseph in a dream, saying, "Arise, take the young Child and His mother, and escape to Egypt, and stay there until I bring you word. For Herod will seek the young Child to kill Him."

The early apostles faced plenty of persecution. You can read about it in the Book of Acts. They were stoned, shipwrecked, beaten with rods, killed—and thrown in jail. This was the natural manifestation of spiritual warfare against them. Acts 5:17–25 shows how God uses angels to deliver His people who are walking out His purposes:

> Then the high priest and all those who were with him (that is, the sect of the Sadducees) rose up and were filled with jealousy. They seized the apostles and put them in the common prison. But during the night an angel of the Lord opened the prison doors and led them out, and said, "Go, stand and speak in the temple to the people all the words of this life."
>
> Having heard this, they entered the temple at dawn and taught.
>
> But the high priest and those who were with him came and called together the Sanhedrin and the senate of all the sons of Israel, and sent to the prison to have them brought out. But when the officers came and did not find them in the prison, they returned and reported, "We found the prison securely shut and the guards standing outside before the doors. But when we opened it, we found no one inside." Now when the high priest, the captain of the temple, and the chief priests heard these things, they were in doubt of what might become of this.
>
> Then one came and told them, "Look, the men whom you put in prison are standing in the temple and teaching the people."

We are in a war, and angels are part of the company of warriors battling principalities, powers, spiritual wickedness in high places, and the rulers of the darkness of this world. We will be more strategic in waging prophetic warfare when we recognize this reality and walk in it. I like the way the late Lester Sumrall, founder of the Lester Sumrall Evangelistic Association, put it in his book *Angels to Help You*:

> In addition to knowing God, angels also know the reality of demons. They know how Lucifer fell from heaven. They observed the many angels who elected to go with him and rebel against God... They know that spiritual warfare is still going on between the forces of God and the forces of Satan, a war that will continue until Satan and his followers are cast into hell for all eternity.
>
> Now, what can we learn from this? I think angels are smarter than we are in regard to how to wage spiritual warfare. They know there is a war on, they are aware of it every day, and they are able to discern the devil's traps.[8]

Again, we will be more strategic in waging prophetic warfare when we recognize there is a war going on—all the time, every day and every night—and stay sensitive enough to the Holy Spirit to discern the devil's traps. We may discern it through a still, small voice, through a vision, or through an angelic encounter. When we wage prophetic warfare, we call all the forces of heaven into play to conquer the mountain the enemy has placed in our path against the will of God.

Chapter 13

SPIRITUAL MAPPING THAT RELEASES PROPHETIC PLANS

I don't know what I did before Google Maps. Actually I do know what I did—I got lost a lot, drove in circles without reaching the intended destination, hit a few dead ends, ran into inconvenient traffic, and wound up frustrated and often late for my appointments. Indeed, I am known for operating in prophetic ministry, but when it comes to directions I seem to have little anointing to drive from A to B without a map.

Merriam-Webster defines a *map* as "a representation usually on a flat surface of the whole or a part of an area."[1] People in every culture use maps in one form or another to lead them and guide them to their destinations. In 2300 BC, Babylonians created maps on clay tablets. Since then, maps have evolved and changed—through medieval times to the Renaissance to, eventually, Google Maps.

Of course, what we see in the natural—the highways, airways, seaways, mountains, and rivers—is only part of the mapping equation. Spiritual mapping is just as real—and just as vital to spiritual warriors—as Google Maps. George Otis Jr., the pioneer of spiritual mapping, defines it as "superimposing our understanding of forces and events in the spiritual domain onto places and circumstances in the material world."[2] And that paves the way for what I call intelligent intercession.

In other words, by understanding how the spiritual realm is influencing the natural realm—and what spirits are the driving forces behind that impact—you can wage more effective prophetic warfare. Although some people take spiritual mapping to extremes—some hyperfocus on the devil—balanced practitioners have advanced in the understanding of this biblical practice and are using the strategy to reveal not only what the enemy is doing but also what God has done and wants to do again.

The bottom line is this: spiritual mapping is a prophetic warfare strategy that can help you discern and break strongholds over your city and open the gates to the King of glory, the Lord strong and mighty. Spiritual mapping goes beyond surface-level prophetic discernment into what is manifesting, and drives down to the root of the issue, which may be ancient. Armed with this intelligence, intercessors can release effective, fervent prayers that over time pile up tremendous power to enforce Christ's victory over enemies that oppose God's will.

Understanding Spiritual Mapping

Otis, who coined the term "spiritual mapping" in the 1990s, told me spiritual mapping and identificational repentance—or what I call spiritual warfare repentance—go hand in hand. As he sees it, individual and corporate repentance are important in the quest for community transformation. But in order for that repentance to be meaningful, we need a full understanding of the issues over which we need to repent.

"Spiritual mapping can reveal the spiritual strongholds that are in place over a particular area and how those strongholds came about through the choices and attitudes and behaviors and sin of the people and of the church," Otis says. "You do the mapping to gain an understanding so you can do something very concrete with that understanding that leads to tangible breakthrough. Outside of that context, spiritual mapping can quite easily evolve into a kind of New Age Mysticism."[3]

Otis also stresses that spiritual mapping is not all about the demonic. When he started teaching the practice, he never intended for people to take such a narrow view. Spiritual mapping, he says, also seeks to understand the purposes and works of God. Spiritual mappers will certainly discover demonic strongholds along the way, but they should also seek to discover the wells that need to be dug again and the old covenants that need to be dusted off.

In his book *Breaking Spiritual Strongholds in Your City,* C. Peter Wagner wrote, "As I see it, spiritual mapping combines research, divine revelation, and confirmatory evidence in order to provide complete and exact data concerning the identity, strategies, and methods employed by spiritual forces of darkness to influence the people and the churches of a given region." He continued, "Spiritual mapping is like the intelligence forces of an army. Through it, we go behind enemy lines to understand the enemy's plans and fortifications."[4]

Nickson Banda, author of *Dynamics of Spiritual Warfare*, writes, "It is spiritual geography showing the routes and operations of the devil...Spiritual Mapping is an exercise of identifying demonic activities operating in an area. Pastor Harold Caballeros of Guatemala City believes that spiritual mapping empowers intercessors in much the same way that x-rays serve physicians. In other words, spiritual mapping is the x-rays [*sic*] of a prayer warrior."[5]

What the Bible Reveals About Spiritual Mapping

There has been some debate in theological circles about the biblical basis for spiritual mapping, but the Bible itself validates the concept. Drawing from Ezekiel 4, Cindy Jacobs, cofounder of Generals International, says, "The spiritual mapping of a city can be used to develop a strategic plan to tear down the strongholds of the enemy."[6] Ezekiel 4:1–3 reads:

> You also, son of man, take a brick and lay it before you and inscribe a city on it, even Jerusalem. Then lay siege against it, and build a fort against it, and build a mound against it; set camps and place battering rams against it all around. Moreover take for yourself an iron plate and set it up for a wall of iron between you and the city. And set your face against it so that it is besieged, and lay siege against it. This shall be a sign to the house of Israel.

We will talk more about the principles and execution of spiritual mapping later in this chapter. For now, focus on the prophetic pattern. God clearly told Ezekiel to make a map of the city on the brick and offered him a prophetic intercession strategy.

Moses's men spied out the land

Ezekiel 4 is not the only scripture that supports spiritual mapping. Consider Moses's warfare wisdom when he sent men to spy out the land of Canaan. The Lord told him to send men to explore the Promised Land, one from each tribe.

> Moses sent them to explore the land of Canaan and said to them, "Go up to this southland, and go up into the mountain. And see what the land is, and the people that dwell in it, whether they are strong or weak, few or many; and what the land is that they dwell in, whether it is good or bad, and what cities are that they dwell in, whether in tents, or in fortifications; and what the land is, whether it is fat or lean, whether there is wood in it or not. And you be courageous and bring some of the fruit of the land."
>
> —Numbers 13:17–20

You know the story. After forty days, the spies came back with a report that the land was flowing with milk and honey and was fruitful. These spiritual mapping forerunners identified the children of Anak and located where the Amalekites, the Hittites, the Jebusites, the Amorites, and the Canaanites dwelled in the land. But the giants and fortified cities intimidated ten of the twelve spies and they declared, "We are not able to go up against the people because they are stronger than we" (Num. 13:31).

This is a good time to point out the realities of spiritual mapping. It is not for the faint of heart. If you are easily intimidated by the spiritual giants in your land—if you don't have faith that the God who displaced principalities and powers, putting them to shame, has given you authority to enforce His victory—then you don't want to venture into the practice of spiritual mapping. In many cities you will discover ancient strongholds that could strike fear in your heart. You will feel like a grasshopper in the face of the spiritual giants (Num. 13:33).

Spiritual mappers need to have a Joshua spirit. Joshua and Caleb went on the same spiritual mapping mission as the other ten spies. When they saw their counterparts withering under a spirit of fear, weeping, and grumbling against Moses and Aaron, they tore their clothes and set the spiritual record straight:

> They spoke to all the assembly of the children of Israel, saying, "The land which we passed through to explore it is a very, very good land. If the LORD delights in us, then He will bring us into this land and give it to us, a land which flows with milk and honey. Only do not rebel against the LORD, nor fear the people of the land because they are bread for us. Their defense is gone from them, and the LORD is with us. Do not fear them."
>
> —NUMBERS 14:7–9

If you are going to wage prophetic warfare strategies, from spiritual mapping to prophetic intercession to waging war with prophecies, you are going to have to trust in the Lord with all your heart and overcome what you see with your natural eyes, or even your spiritual eyes. Remember the saying I learned while on the mission field in Nicaragua, a land where high levels of witchcraft are operating: "A devil exposed is a devil defeated." In other words, if you can see the enemy, you can defeat the enemy. It doesn't matter how big the enemy is or how long he has occupied the land. If you get a prophetic warfare strategy from God, it will always lead you into triumph.

Nehemiah was knee deep

Nehemiah was knee deep in spiritual mapping. He arose at night with a few men, telling no one what God had put in his heart to do for Jerusalem—to rebuild the walls of the city. Like the twelve Israelites in Moses's day, Nehemiah went with a small crew to spy out the land. We read the account of his mapping exercise in Nehemiah 2:13–16:

> So I went out by night by the Valley Gate toward the Dragon's Well and then to the Dung Gate, because I was inspecting the broken-down walls of Jerusalem and its burned gates. Next I passed by the Fountain Gate and then to the King's Pool, but there was no place for my mount to pass. By going up along the riverbed at night, I inspected the wall. Then I turned back so that I could enter by the Valley Gate, and then came back again. The officials did not know where I went or what I did, since I had not yet told it to the Jews, the priests, the nobles, the officials, or to any of the others who would do the work.

Though he could have started at any gate, I believe Nehemiah intentionally started his mapping at the Valley Gate. This is significant because it was the site where Manasseh, a former king of Judah, welcomed idolatry into the city. Manasseh was so steeped in idolatry and spiritual immorality that he sacrificed his own son in the fire, practiced divination, sought omens, and consulted mediums and spiritists in the valley of Hinnom (2 Kings 21:6). The Valley Gate was a symbol of rebellion. Nehemiah's team would eventually restore that gate in an act of obedience to God, redeeming it. We will talk more about gates later in this chapter.

Joshua mapped the Promised Land

When all of Israel was assembled at Shiloh to possess the Promised Land, Joshua instructed the camp to choose three men from each tribe to go out through the land and essentially map it, describing the land in seven portions. Let's listen in to this account:

> So the men got up and left. Joshua commanded those who were leaving to survey the land, saying, "Go and walk back and forth throughout the land. Write a description of it, then return to me. Here in Shiloh I will cast lots for you before the LORD." The men went and passed through the land. In a book they wrote a description of it by cities in seven portions, and they came back to Joshua at the Shiloh settlement. Joshua cast lots for them in Shiloh before the LORD. There Joshua apportioned the land for the children of Israel according to their divisions.
>
> —JOSHUA 18:8–10

From there the Bible goes on to offer detailed descriptions of the information the men brought back about borders, hills, spring waters, slopes, and cities and villages. Each tribe knew its God-given territory, and tribe members would fight to the end to protect the promise of God to their people against enemy intruders. In a spiritual context, we must know the territory God has placed us in and protect it from spiritual enemies that have invaded or are invading. As the Israelites did, we must dispossess the former occupants. That means encountering territorial spirits, demons that rule over geographic areas. Angels can also be territorial spirits.

Paul surveyed the gods

Spiritual mapping examples are not confined to the Old Testament. We see Paul the apostle doing some loose spiritual mapping of his own while he was waiting for his missionary team to join him in Athens. The Bible says as he waited, "his spirit was provoked within him as he saw that the city was full of idols" (Acts 17:16). With the wisdom of the Holy Spirit, Paul mapped the city spiritually as he walked through the streets and used the intelligence he gathered as an evangelism strategy.

> Then Paul stood in the middle of the Areopagus, and said: "Men of Athens, I perceive that in all things you are very religious. For as I passed by and looked up at your objects of worship, I found an altar with this inscription:
>
> TO THE UNKNOWN GOD.
>
> Whom you therefore unknowingly worship, Him I proclaim to you.
>
> "God who made the world and all things in it, being Lord of heaven and earth, does not live in temples made by hands."
>
> —Acts 17:22–24

Spiritual mapping always has a purpose. Spiritual mapping helps us discern the strongholds—whether ancient or more recently established—in a city or territory. Spiritual mapping can uncover the destiny of God over a region. Spiritual mapping takes work. It's not all about praying for God to reveal what is operating; it's also about studying the history of your region.

Principles of Spiritual Mapping

Armed with an understanding of what spiritual mapping is and biblical examples to support the initiative, let's move into the spiritual principles of the practice. God worked with Ezekiel on a prophetic pattern for spiritual mapping found in Scripture that gives us a broad overview of the process. Ezekiel 4 shows how Ezekiel followed God's instructions to lay siege to Jerusalem.

Seeing transformation come to your city or region starts with making a spiritual map. Ezekiel 4:1 says, "You also, son of man, take a brick and lay it before you and inscribe a city on it, even Jerusalem." Without a spiritual map, we may find some success in pushing back darkness through discernment and clues the Holy Spirit shares, but if we want to see the King of glory resume His rightful position, we need to go deeper. Spiritual mapping that reveals strongholds helps us accomplish that goal.

Next, Ezekiel modeled the strategy to defeat the enemy. Ezekiel 4:2 says, "Then lay siege against it, and build a fort against it, and build a mound against it; set camps and place battering rams against it all around." Essentially, Ezekiel built small forts around the map he made representing the besiegers (or, in our language, intercessors) that would surround the city. Watchmen would climb up into the forts and spy out the land, giving information back to the intercessors to do spiritual battle. Unified prayer is the battering ram against the enemy's strongholds.

Finally, God told Ezekiel to build a wall. Ezekiel 4:3 says, "Moreover take for yourself an iron plate and set it up for a wall of iron between you and the city. And set your face against it so that it is besieged, and lay siege against it. This shall be a sign to the house of Israel." This part of the strategy is vital as you set out to use your spiritual map as a guide to lay siege to your city for the Lord. The wall protects the intercessors from the enemy's flaming missiles. Intercessors must not think the enemy is easily going to hand over land he has been occupying.

It is vital that intercessors go into the siege with repentance and claiming Psalm 91 so they can withstand the backlash against any move to bring healing to the land. Wisdom dictates having intercessors in the background praying for the intercessors on the front lines laying siege against the city. Let me be clear: This is not something you should attempt to do on your own. This is a corporate prayer strategy that takes time to execute. It is a fierce tug-of-war with spiritual enemies who aren't going to let go of the rope easily. You are going to have to yank it from their thieving hands with the power of the Holy Spirit.

The How-To of Spiritual Mapping

Now it's time to get down to the nuts and bolts—the nitty-gritty how-to—of spiritual mapping. I'll warn you up front—it's a lot of work. You may spend hours researching online and may even need to make a trip to your local library. You may need to interview believers who have lived in the community for sixty or seventy years and witnessed past moves of God and the increase of darkness in the community over time.

Spiritual mapping is a practical exercise but one done with prayer and discernment. At the onset ask the Holy Spirit to lead you and guide you to the truth that will arm your intercessory prayer team to set the captives free. Generally speaking you are looking for research that reveals the spiritual condition of churches in your area. Barna Group has some overarching research that can offer clues, and the American Bible Society puts out an annual report about Bible-minded cities that could help you get the big picture of Christianity at large and the state of various cities.

Also look for patterns of sin in your region as a sign of demonic activity. In my state, Florida, we have one of the largest LGBT populations in the country.[7] We also have high crime rates and high drug and alcohol abuse rates,[8] and it is widely known that we house the psychic capital of the world.[9] Twelve of the nation's one hundred most dangerous cities are in Florida, according to Neighborhoodscout.com,[10] and the Centers for Disease Control reports Florida is seeing the highest number of new HIV cases in the nation.[11]

Look for the patterns in your city. There could be strongholds of child abuse, divorce, unemployment, poverty, disease, apathy, or something else that is demonically inspired. Look for the sin in the city, from immorality to idolatry to adultery and beyond. Look for any signs of demonic activity in the community, its marketplaces, its schools, and even its churches. The Interstate 4 Corridor—a highway that runs from Daytona Beach through Orlando and into Tampa—has a high rate of pastors falling into adultery and some even committing suicide.[12]

Stay up to date with the news in your area. The headlines tip the devil's hand. Some of the major sins that pollute the land—and from which the land must be healed after warfare repentance and a battle against principalities and powers that are influencing the minds and hearts of the people in a region—are idolatry, immorality, bloodshed, and broken covenant. Look for the root of these sins in your region. Map them out.

Questions You Should Ask

John Dawson, founder of the International Reconciliation Coalition, a global network dedicated to healing wounds between people groups and elements of society, wrote a strategic book called *Taking Our Cities for God: How to Break Spiritual Strongholds.* In it he suggests a list of twenty questions that can get you started on your spiritual mapping journey:

1. What place does your city have in this nation's history?
2. Was there ever the imposition of a new culture or language through conquest?
3. What were the religious practices of ancient peoples on the site?
4. Was there a time when a new religion emerged?
5. Under what circumstances did the gospel first enter the city?
6. Has the national or city government ever disintegrated?
7. What has been the leadership style of past governments?
8. Have there ever been wars that affected this city?...
9. Was the city itself the site of a battle?
10. What names have been used to label the city, and what are their meanings?
11. Why was the city originally settled?
12. Did the city have a founder? What was his dream?
13. As political, military and religious leaders emerged, what did they dream for themselves and for the city?

14. What political, economic and religious institutions have dominated the life of the city?
15. What has been the experience of immigrants to the city?
16. Have there been any traumatic experiences such as economic collapse, race riots or an earthquake?
17. Did the city ever experience the birth of a socially transforming technology?
18. Has there ever been the sudden opportunity to create wealth such as the discovery of oil or a new irrigation technology?
19. Has there ever been religious conflict among competing religions or among Christians?
20. What is the history of relationships among the races?[13]

I will add to this list a few more things to consider:

1. How has God moved in this region in the past? Have there been revivals or outpourings?
2. What great men and women of God from past generations have sown into the spirit in the region?
3. What spiritual encampments has the enemy set up through false religion in the territory? How long have they been established?
4. What type of occult activity is present in the area? Beyond psychic shops, are their New Agers, Kabbalah centers, witches' meetings, etc.?

5. What manner of sexual immorality is dominant in your area (porn shops and strip clubs, for example)?
6. Is there a Masonic stronghold in your area?
7. Are there frequent tragedies or rising crime?
8. What is the mayor's vision for the city going forward?
9. What is the history of Christianity in the city?
10. How is the school system performing?
11. What is the state of the local economy? Is it thriving, or are businesses shutting down? Is unemployment high or low?
12. Where are the gates in your city? Those may be literal gates or physical gates such as ports or the entrance to a city; or they could be spiritual gates such as churches, occult centers, etc.

You will probably come up with additional questions and areas of research as you start the journey. The idea is to dive in and get started. Look for someone with special skill sets in the area of research and assign him or her as the head of the team, with volunteers working alongside. What you uncover could be disturbing, or it could be exciting if you find that God moved in mighty ways in decades past.

Once you have your answers, develop a prayer strategy to take down these spiritual strongholds one by one, or break into intercessory prayer teams and assign each team to wage prophetic warfare against a specific area of concern. Don't stop there. Actively look for the change you are believing to see. It probably won't happen overnight, but with God on your side and your effective, fervent prayers, you will chip away at the demonic rocks in your region so the King of glory can take His place once again.

Spiritual Mapping–Driven Breakthroughs

Spiritual mapping has facilitated full-blown transforming revival in communities like Fiji. The Sentinel Group calls this Journey to Transformation; it is a process that is designed to prepare a community for divine visitation and subsequent societal transformation—a condition otherwise known as spiritual awakening. That journey includes spiritual mapping.

According to a report from The Sentinel Group, the village of Nataleira, Fiji, was "paradise gone wrong." The village had no fresh water and a dead coral reef. Many of the young people in the village had committed suicide as well. Things changed when the 1,200 locals turned to God in repentance and even dedicated their land to God. Within a couple days a light appeared over the coast. Then the reef came alive and "thousands of fish were swimming in the shallows."[14]

According to Otis, "We have seen in case after case after case after case after case of people going into personal repentance followed by informed corporate repentance fed by spiritual mapping that has led to remarkable transformation of these communities with signs and wonders." Otis continued: "When we're talking about sin, time doesn't heal things. Spiritual wounds are healed not by time but by repentance—and you have to go back and close these doors and windows and make things right."[15]

CHAPTER 14

PROPHETIC PRAYER WALKS AND MARCHES

FOR NEARLY TWO hundred years Clay County, Kentucky, was marked by violent family feuds, moonshining, murder, extreme poverty, government corruption, and deadly drug abuse. Clay County—and specifically the city of Manchester—made national headlines over and over again for all the wrong reasons.

In July 1989 *USA Today* reported that over forty percent of Clay County's population was growing marijuana and the Daniel Boone National Forest had become a pot field.[1] By the turn of the century the area moved on to a new drug of choice. The *Lexington Herald-Leader* dubbed it "The Painkiller Capital of America" in January 2003 as OxyContin was sold on nearly every street corner.[2] From there, "cooks" and crooks rose up to manufacture methamphetamine, a crystalline drug that can be snorted, smoked, or injected.

Political officials and police were being paid to look the other way. The drug lords bought the elections every four years. Over ninety percent of the county's high school students were strung out on one drug or another. Overdoses became a common occurrence, with memorial crosses strewn along the city streets like a picket fence. Meanwhile, the pastors were polarized based on doctrinal differences and felt hopeless to help members whose families were drug-addicted and dying.[3]

"Our kids started dying. Out of desperation, we started praying in the fall of 2003. We started crying out to the Lord. A Southern Baptist preacher named Ken Bollin had a dream," says Doug Abner, who was pastoring a church in Manchester at the time. "Ken wanted to have a march against drugs and corruption on May 2, 2004. We received threats on our lives, our homes, and our churches but we knew it was God."[4]

The morning of May 2, in the pouring rain, four thousand people turned out for the prayer march. Manchester is only home to two thousand people. The prayer walk rally ended at a park. There the pastors and church leaders repented for being more concerned about their own denominations, their own congregations, and their own programs than the lost souls in Clay County. When they asked the people to forgive them and vowed to work together, Abner says the manifest presence of the Lord fell in the park to the degree that people could hardly breathe.[5]

"The fear of the Lord gripped the community. Drug dealers and corrupt politicians began to tell on each other," Abner says. "A few months later, the FBI came to town and started arresting people. Eventually, they arrested the mayor and the assistant police chief, the fire chief, the 911 director, several local judges and city council members, a circuit judge, school board members and the superintendent and lots of others. They arrested the drug dealers, who were selling drugs to the nation from Manchester."[6]

Today, Manchester is known as the City of Hope. God even healed the land. For years, the water tasted foul unless you used a water filter. In 2008, Clay County's water won first place in Kentucky's municipal water system for its taste. After years of streams without fish, suddenly big fish came back. Manchester is now home to fishing tournaments. The forests were barren, but now the bears, turkeys, and elk have returned.

(Clay County now has one of the largest elk populations in the country.)[7] Churches and local businesses banded together with the court system to develop second-chance employment programs for Clay County's population of recovering drug addicts. As the economy improved, new businesses started opening to provide those jobs.

"I asked the Lord, 'Why Manchester?' And He said, 'Because I want the world to see what can happen when people get desperate and begin to come together,'" Abner says. "As bad as the darkness was, our biggest problem was not the darkness. Our biggest problem was the lack of light—the church not being what it is supposed to be. When we came together in desperation, He healed the land. He changed the fabric of our society."[8]

What We Can Learn From Joshua

Abner and Bollin took a page out of Joshua's prophetic warfare plans—and so can we. Indeed, perhaps the best known prophetic prayer march was at the Battle of Jericho in Joshua 6. The Bible says Jericho was tightly secured—no one was going in and no one was coming out. Despite the fact that Jericho was a mighty fortress, God told Joshua He was delivering the city into his hands. God gave him the battle plan:

> All the men of fighting age shall march around the city. Circle the city once. Do this for six days. Seven priests shall carry seven ram's horn trumpets before the ark. On the seventh day, march around the city seven times, with the priests blowing the trumpets. When they blow a long blast on the ram's horn and when you hear the trumpet sound, all the people shall shout a loud battle cry. The walls of the city will fall down, and the people will go up, every man straight ahead.
>
> —Joshua 6:3–5

Joshua took great care to make sure the priests and army understood, even clarifying this important point: "Do not shout a battle cry, and do not let your voices be heard. Do not let a word come out of your mouths until the time I say to you, 'Shout the battle cry!' Then shout" (Josh. 6:10–11). This plan required patience and precision. I do not believe the prophetic warfare strategy would have worked if Joshua had taken two days off in the middle to rest or marched around the wall only six times on the seventh day. The conclusion of the matter:

> So the people shouted, and they blew the trumpets. When the people heard the trumpet sound, they shouted a loud battle cry, and the wall fell down. So the people went up into the city, one man after the other, and they captured it. They destroyed all that was in the city: man and woman, young and old, and oxen, sheep, and donkey with the edge of the sword.
>
> —Joshua 6:20–21

We can learn several vital lessons about prophetic warfare strategies from Joshua's plight. First, Joshua didn't have to come up with a battle plan on his own. This is a good lesson for us all to learn because the Spirit of God should always be the source of our prophetic warfare strategies. If we run into battle without His leading, we could end up running into the heart of a war He hasn't called us to fight.

Paul, speaking by the inspiration of the Holy Spirit, gave thanks to "God who always causes us to triumph in Christ and through us reveals the fragrance of His knowledge in every place" (2 Cor. 2:14). God causes us to triumph in Christ—and the keywords are "in Christ." When we run ahead of Christ, we can get into serious trouble. Thank God, He will bail us out; but wisdom relies on the Spirit of God to take us into and through the battle. We will look more closely at the "shall I go up" factor later in this chapter.

Second, Joshua executed the plan perfectly. This is another good lesson for us because God's plans are perfect. If we insert our own fears or our own ideas into God's well-laid plans, things may not wind up the way He intended. God's thoughts are higher than our thoughts; His ways are higher than our ways—and His battle plans are better than our battle plans (Isa. 55:9). When God gives us a specific strategy, we need to execute it exactly as it was given if we want to see its intended supernatural results. The overarching lesson is this: victory in battle demands obedience to the Word of God. You can't compromise, dilute, or water down the Word of God and expect it to work at full strength. As spiritual warriors, we often quote 2 Corinthians 10. We cheer about verses 3 through 5:

> For though we walk in the flesh, we do not war according to the flesh. For the weapons of our warfare are not carnal, but mighty through God to the pulling down of strongholds, casting down imaginations and every high thing that exalts itself against the knowledge of God, bringing every thought into captivity to the obedience of Christ…

Sometimes, we forget about verse 6:

> …and being ready to punish all disobedience when your obedience is complete.

That is another way, essentially, of saying "submit yourselves to God. Resist the devil, and he will flee" (James 4:7). Put still another way, you cannot take authority over the devil if you are out of alignment with the Word of God, whether the written word or a prophetic warfare strategy. Success in

Christ is connected to obedience to Christ, the Word made flesh (John 1:14).

Moses's Prophetic Warfare March

Beyond Jericho there are plenty of other prophetic warfare marches in the Bible (which validates this strategy as the Bible says that by "two or three witnesses shall every word be established" [2 Cor. 13:1]).

Just before the Exodus march we find the Egyptian army overtaking the Israelites camping by the sea. The children of Israel were trapped between the Red Sea on one side and a sea of Egyptians marching toward them on the other side—and the voice of fear terrified their souls. Giving in to the voice of fear, they turned on Moses and accused him of bringing them out to the wilderness to die.

That did not faze Moses, who spoke words of life:

> Fear not! Stand firm! And see the salvation of the Lord, which He will show you today. For the Egyptians whom you have seen today, you shall never see again. The Lord shall fight for you, while you hold your peace.
>
> —Exodus 14:13–14

Then Moses got the prophetic warfare strategy:

> The Lord said to Moses…"Speak to the children of Israel, so that they go forward. And as for you, lift up your rod, and stretch out your hand over the sea, and divide it; then the children of Israel shall go on dry ground through the midst of the sea. As for Me, surely, I will harden the hearts of the Egyptians, so that they shall follow them, and I will be honored through Pharaoh, through all his army, his chariots, and his horsemen. Then the Egyptians shall know that I am the

> LORD when I am honored through Pharaoh, his chariots, and his horsemen."
>
> —EXODUS 14:15–18

You know the end of the story about this prophetic warfare march. Moses obeyed God, and the children of Israel went into the midst of the sea on dry ground with the waters forming walls on either side of them. When the Egyptians tried to chase them down, Moses stretched out his hand over the sea and the waters closed up on them.

As was the case with Joshua's march, we can learn several key lessons from Moses's leadership during this crisis. First, Moses had enough faith in God not to panic in the midst of the enemy onslaught. Many people get overwhelmed with the spiritual warfare, isolate themselves, and feed the flesh, hoping the storm will pass, instead of rising up against the voice of fear that tells them they can't win.

Moses did not give in to the accusations or the fear. He inclined his ear to the God who delivers. Moses also recalled the prophetic promises God had given him and the many miracles God had performed on his behalf. To the children of Israel's credit, they didn't have an encounter with God at the burning bush to spark their faith—but they did see the mighty hand of God move during the ten plagues. The Israelites should have ultimately believed God but faltered in the face of what looked like impossible circumstances.

Because they were frightened and faithless, Moses pointed them to the Lord and said, "Hold your peace" (Exod. 14:14). The Hebrew word *peace* in this verse means "to be silent, be dumb, be speechless, be deaf."[9] That is interesting because Moses's ultimate instruction to the Israelites wasn't merely not to say anything, but not to hear anything. In other words, he was admonishing them not to give ear to the voice of fear, and by all means not to speak it out of their mouths.

Finally, we learn from this event that God partners with us in warfare. Although Moses told the Israelites, "The Lord shall fight for you," he also had a part to play (Exod. 14:14). Yes, the Lord did fight for them, but it was through Moses's obedience to follow the prophetic warfare instruction. If Moses had not stretched forth his hand, God may not have parted and subsequently closed the Red Sea. God will always do His part, but He won't do our part. God is sovereign and can do whatever He chooses whenever He chooses, but He chooses most often to partner with us to accomplish His will and to obtain victory over His enemies.

Shall I Go Up?

"Shall I go up?" David, a mighty warrior for God, asked Jehovah this critical question before running to the battle line—and we would be wise to do the same. In the realm of prophetic warfare strategies, this is a baseline question.

Although we war from a place of victory, rushing into spiritual warfare outside of God's timing can lead to defeat. Although we are taught to remain on the offensive, presuming to enter a battle God has not called us to fight can be a dangerous mistake. And although we are in a spiritual war, the battle really is the Lord's.

"Shall I go up?" Every spiritual warrior needs to ask this question before engaging the enemy. In other words we need to be led by the Holy Spirit into battle if we want God to lead us into triumph. If we lose a battle, it could very well be that the Holy Spirit didn't lead us into the spiritual skirmish in the first place.

Again, David was a mighty warrior for God. He officially started his military career by defeating a giant named Goliath who terrified the entire Israeli army (1 Sam. 17). Talk about coming onto the warfare scene with a flare!

David built quite a reputation for warfare. In fact, after David defeated Goliath, Saul set the brave teenager over his men of war. When David was coming home from his big win, the women came out of all the cities of Israel. They were singing and dancing and said, "Saul has slain his thousands, and David his ten thousands" (1 Sam. 18:7).

David could have gotten puffed up in the midst of the honor. He could have taken pride in his hand-to-hand combat skills. But he didn't get prideful, and he didn't get presumptuous. And soon enough David would have the opportunity to play hero again when the Philistines were fighting against the city of Keilah and robbing the threshing floors (1 Sam 23:1).

Clearly there was an injustice underway, but David didn't take it upon himself to bring justice. Rather, he asked his just God this critical question: "'Shall I go and attack these Philistines?' And the Lord said to David, 'Go and attack the Philistines, and rescue Keilah'" (1 Sam. 23:2).

David's men admitted they were afraid to go to battle, but David wasn't prideful and presumptuous enough to think he could save the whole city with a sling and a stone just because he had done it once before. And he didn't pooh-pooh their fears. Instead, David inquired of the Lord a second time. The Lord gave David the confirmation he was looking for:

> And the Lord answered him and said, "Arise, go down to Keilah because I am giving the Philistines into your hand." Then David and his men went to Keilah. He fought with the Philistines and carried off their livestock, and he struck them with a great slaughter. So David rescued the inhabitants of Keilah.
>
> —1 Samuel 23:4–5

There is a good lesson here. Even though God initially told David to go up, David was cautious—and humble enough—to continue seeking the Lord for confirmation when it appeared the circumstances were changing. He was concerned for the welfare of his men, who were afraid. Instead of rebuking them for flowing in fear, he went back to the Lord to make sure he'd heard right.

I believe this careful, caring approach is one of the reasons David's men trusted his leadership so much. If you want to be an effective general in God's army, you need to pray about your team's legitimate concerns before heading into battle. That doesn't mean you cower in the face of a challenge. It just means you make doubly—even triply—sure that you are in God's will and that you have counted the costs of waging war before leading others into dangerous territory.

Later, when David was anointed king over Israel, he once again faced the prospect of war. The Philistines heard he was officially installed as king and went down to the stronghold, ready to attack. "So David asked the LORD, 'Shall I go up against the Philistines? Will You give them into my hand?' The LORD said to David, 'Go up, because I will certainly give them into your hand'" (2 Sam. 5:19). David defeated the Philistines and gave God the glory, saying, "The LORD has breached my enemies before me like bursting tides" (2 Sam. 5:20).

There was a time, though, that David was not supposed to "go up." And if he had moved without the Lord's prophetic warfare strategy, it could have brought great defeat upon Israel. These next verses show David's wisdom and dependence on God in warfare. When the Philistines went up and spread out in the Valley of Rephaim, David could have presumed he was supposed to go to battle because of the many victories. Instead, David asked the Lord:

> When David inquired of the LORD, He said, "You shall not go up. Circle around behind them and come against them opposite the trees. When you hear the sound of

> marching in the tops of the trees, pay attention, because at that point the LORD is going before you to defeat the army of the Philistines."
>
> —2 SAMUEL 5:23–24

This time marching was involved, but it wasn't David or the Israelites who marched into battle. The Lord did the marching and the fighting. Although ultimately the battle is always the Lord's, we are His battle-axes. He can get the job done without us, and sometimes does, but our obedience is still part of the equation for ultimate victory. David could have seen great losses if he had neglected to incline his ear to the Lord and heed the prophetic warfare strategy.

Before you run to the battle line, ask the Holy Spirit, "Shall I go up?" Then obey what He tells you. It could be that He has assigned someone else to "go up" and defeat the enemy; it could be that God is taking the battle into His own hands; or it could be that you aren't yet skilled enough in battle to take on the enemy that is rising up. The reason doesn't matter. What matters is that we stay in the will of God, even in our spiritual warfare.

PRAYER WALKING: ON-SITE INTERCESSION

Marching is one thing; prayer walking is another. Although many people involved in marches like the pro-life movement March for Life surely pray as they are marching, prayer walking takes the concept a step further—or should I say a couple of steps fewer. The idea is not to march a long distance but to target a specific area to walk around and pray on-site. The simplest definition of *prayer walking* is "walking around a specific area of concern and praying."

Steve Hawthorne and Graham Kendrick, authors of *Prayerwalking: Praying On Site with Insight*, believe prayer walking and praying on-site can help intercessors in these four ways: thaw the ice in your neighborhood; overcome fear; contend with evil; and progress in prayer. I will summarize each thought:

1. "Thaw the ice . . . Prayerwalking provides a quiet way to help people while gradually coming to understand and care for them," Hawthorne and Kendrick write. "The climate of steady prayer can warm the atmosphere of friendship. Hearts opened by prayer can lead to doors opened for God's healing touch."[10]

2. "Overcome fear . . . Most believers are genuinely concerned about their city but find themselves inhibited by fears and habits of isolation. Why endure the unsettled feeling that you don't belong in your own city? Or the nagging guilt that you should do something?" the authors ask. "Prayerwalking provides a way to re-enter your inner city with godly confidence."[11]

3. "Contend with evil. Many Christians feel besieged by evil. Rising crime and open hostility to Christ appear to be energized by stubborn spiritual evil," they write. "Prayerwalking provides a way to wage some of the necessary spiritual war with your feet literally on the ground."[12]

4. "Progress in prayer. Most Christians sincerely desire to pray more," they write. "But who hasn't found it hard to build a life of prayer? Prayerwalking offers struggling intercessors one stimulating way to stretch themselves in prayer."[13]

One of the most extreme examples of a prayer-walking intercessor is Lyn Hanush, who walked across America with two other intercessors for God and country. The ladies walked from Blaine, Washington, to Key West, Florida—over 4,000 miles—in one year, two months, eleven days, and six hours.[14] "It's got to be done, and it has to be praying for our nation—for the unity of our country," Lyn told CBN.com. "I believe that God had called me to walk and pray, and to claim this land step by step back for Him."[15]

Of course, you don't have to walk across the nation to make a significant impact with your intercession. You can start in your neighborhood, at your child's school, in your workplace, at the city hall—wherever God is leading you.

Effective Prayer Walking 101

A number of authoritative books have been written on the topic of prayer walking, but street warriors can get started with these best practices:

1. **Know your city.** Take the time to discover the history of your city. What you unearth could reveal demonic strongholds from history. You could discover patterns of murder or abuse for which you need to engage the identificational repentance strategy we discuss in chapter 15. You can research the "gates" of the city, where people and things come in and out. Once armed with an understanding of the issues past and present in your city—including knowledge of sites where sin dominates, where tragedy struck, where natural wars were fought, etc.—you can seek the Lord for His on-site prayer strategy.

2. **Search for prophetic words over your region.** God has a plan and purpose for each and every city. Do some research to discover any prophetic words spoken over your city or even specific places in your city. We discussed waging warfare with prophetic words in an earlier chapter. Going to the site the prophecy speaks of and declaring and praying through the prophetic word is powerful.

3. **Pray before you walk.** Prayer walking is all about praying and walking, but you should pray before you walk. You need strategy and insight about when, where, and how to pray. You will want to prepare your heart, which may lead you into personal repentance and/or fasting.

4. **Search the Word of God.** Part of any effective prayer strategy is employing scriptures. Study the Word of God for the most appropriate scriptures to apply to your prayer walk. For example, Luke 1:17 is good for turning hearts to God; 2 Chronicles 7:14 works well if you are seeking to heal the land; Revelation 12:9–12 is appropriate for exposing Satan's schemes in a city; and Jeremiah 29:7 is a strong prayer for peace in the city.

5. **Be practical.** On the practical front, prayer walkers should try not to draw attention to themselves. This is different than a march, which may include prayer walking but is purposed to make a statement to onlookers. With safety in mind, walk against the traffic if you are on a major road. And of course, wear

comfortable clothing and bring along something to record any revelations you receive during the prayer walk, such as a pen and paper or your smartphone. Finally, debrief after the prayer walk to make sure your team unpacks any important observations or revelations.

You probably won't see immediate results of your prayer walking efforts, but you can know this: if God is calling you to do it, then the endeavor will be fruitful. If you pray according to the Scriptures, you can be sure God is working: "So shall My word be that goes forth from My mouth; it shall not return to Me void, but it shall accomplish that which I please, and it shall prosper in the thing for which I sent it" (Isa. 55:11).

Chapter 15

WHEN REPENTANCE IS WARFARE

Although David goes down in biblical history as a man after God's own heart, Daniel had his own battle with the lions that demonstrated his complete trust in God. The prophet Daniel was gifted and faithful; he walked with integrity in a corrupt culture that tempted him to compromise the call of God on his life.

In other words Daniel did not practice sin. Daniel stood firmly against idolatry, loving not his life even unto death if that's what it took. Daniel was filled with knowledge, skill, and understanding—and he understood the power of repenting for sins he did not commit to deliver a nation out of enemy bondage.

Daniel was a man who walked in the Spirit on his knees. Three times a day he fell to the ground, prayed, and gave thanks to God in plain sight of a Babylonian government that outlawed making appeals to heaven.

The Bible doesn't tell us much about what Daniel prayed, but we know that he was steady in the calling, he was responsive to the burden, and he set aside a time and place to pray three times a day. I believe Daniel prayed what was on the Lord's heart in that hour. I believe he partnered with Jehovah to see a nation delivered from evil—and he did it, at least in part, through identificational repentance.

Identificational repentance is a term John Dawson, author of *Healing America's Wounds*, coined in the 1990s. It simply refers to a type of prayer that identifies with and confesses the sins of one's nation, city, people group, church, or family before God.[1] Until Dawson's book dusted off this ancient revelation, few practiced this powerful prophetic warfare strategy.

Understanding Identificational Repentance

We should go into prophetic warfare with a heart of repentance, renouncing any agreement with the enemy over which we are taking authority—we will go deeper into that later in this chapter. But there is another side to the repentance coin: identificational repentance.

Again, Dawson defines *identificational repentance* as "a type of prayer that identifies with and confesses the sins of one's nation, city, people group, church, or family before God." But let's break this down further. *Oxford Dictionary* defines *identificational* as "relating to or involving identification."[2] *Identification* is "the action or process of identifying someone or something or the fact of being identified."[3]

C. Peter Wagner calls this the power to heal the past.[4] I call it warfare repentance because it strips Satan's right to operate. When you can identify what gave or is giving the devil a right to hold back God's will and blessing, you can lay the axe to its root. It takes a prophetic spirit to identify these issues. We can make blanket repentance to the Lord, and if we lack understanding and insight, this act could take us into revelation because the Lord loves a contrite heart. But ultimately we need the Holy Spirit's help to identify those things for which we need to repent. This is true at the personal and corporate levels.

For balance's sake we also need to understand that every issue we come against is not rooted in a need to repent. The enemy can attack where there are open doors of hidden sin and iniquity, but he can also attack those with clean hands and a pure heart. The Holy Spirit must lead us into warfare repentance, or we are just beating the air. Repentance is never a bad place to start, then, but it may not be the prophetic warfare strategy that will bring the ultimate breakthrough.

In the realm of warfare repentance, we repent over sin for which we may have played no direct role. You may have attended a prayer meeting where people were repenting for slavery even though it took place over one hundred years before they were born. You may have heard people repenting for abortions even though they had never had an abortion. You may have heard people repenting for immorality even though they were pure. The shed blood of Christ on Calvary best demonstrates the concept of identificational repentance. Jesus took on the sin of the world and paid the price for that sin even though He was sinless.

Identificational repentance goes back to move forward. Warfare repentance zeros in on the enemy's entry path and slams the door shut. It is important to recognize that even though spiritual warfare and intercessory circles picked up on this in the 1990s, it is not new. Solomon assured us there is nothing new under the sun. In different times and in different generations the body of Christ has seen an emphasis on identificational repentance, which I am now reclaiming as prophetic warfare repentance during a time when the body is picking up old weapons for a new season.

Beyond Daniel, Ezekiel, Nehemiah, and some others whose intercessory prayer practices we will look at in this chapter, we can turn to the pages of more modern history to see examples of identificational repentance. They didn't use those terms, but they tapped into the same power Daniel and other prophets understood.

In the 1559 *Book of Common Prayer*, also known as the Elizabethan Prayer Book, we find this prayer: "Remember not,

Lord, our iniquities, nor the iniquities of our forefathers: Spare us, good Lord, spare thy people, whom thou hast redeemed with thy most precious blood, and be not angry with us for ever...Lord, have mercy upon us. Christ, have mercy upon us. Lord, have mercy upon us."[5]

Noteworthy is the fact that this was the third revision for the Anglican Church and was published after Queen Elizabeth I ascended to Britain's throne. The Anglican Church was restored during her reign after the Catholic Queen Mary ruled for six years. Queen Elizabeth ushered the nation back toward Jesus as the only mediator, forsaking the sin of worshipping idols.[6]

As you see, this is not just a Pentecostal-Charismatic practice. *The Book of Occasional Services* of the Episcopal Church, USA, also contains a prayer of corporate confession of generational sin: "Teach your Church, O Lord, to mourn the sins of which it is guilty, and to repent and forsake them; that, by your pardoning grace, the results of our iniquities may not be visited upon our children and our children's children; through Jesus Christ our Lord. Amen."[7]

We pray 2 Chronicles 7:14 plenty in the modern-day prayer movement, but we don't always look at the greater context. I believe that is one of the reasons why we have seen so little fruit from this strategy. If you pull back the lens and look at the bigger picture of this prophetic word, you will see that Solomon had just dedicated the temple for which David had given him the blueprints. The Lord actually appeared to Solomon at night and told the king He had heard his prayer.

Based on the verse preceding it, 2 Chronicles 7:14 is a prayer for an appointed time and season: "When I shut up the heaven and there is no rain, or when I command the locusts to devour the land, or send pestilence on My people..." (2 Chron. 7:13). Second Chronicles 7:14, then, is most effective in times of judgment—when judgment has already manifested. This is not a strategy you employ to stave off judgment—praying for mercy is the right strategy to potentially move God's heart after judgment has fallen.

Warfare repentance is part of seeking the mercy of God in order to stave off judgment, so God doesn't strike the land. It is also part of the strategy for walking out 2 Chronicles 7:14, so God will heal the land. If we were spiritually keen enough to press into warfare repentance, we might see less discipline on our nation. Of course, that is not the only answer. Preaching the gospel, demonstrating signs and wonders to hard hearts, and engaging in intercessory prayer are all part of the synergy we need to tap.

Personal Repentance: Going In Clean

There can be no prophetic warfare repentance without personal repentance. When we engage in prophetic warfare repentance, we tap into a supernatural repentance that leads to a supernatural deliverance through breaking supernatural ties with principalities, powers, rulers of darkness, and spiritual wickedness in high places. We need to go into warfare repentance cleansed of our own personal sin by the blood of Jesus.

"Who may ascend the mountain of the Lord? Who may stand in his holy place? The one who has clean hands and a pure heart, who does not trust in an idol or swear by a false god. He will receive the blessing from the Lord and vindication from God their Savior" (Ps. 24:3–5, niv). And Proverbs 28:13 says, "He who covers his sins will not prosper, but whoever confesses and forsakes them will have mercy."

When John the Baptist preached, "Repent, for the kingdom of heaven is at hand" (Matt. 3:2), that word *repent* came from the Greek word *metanoeó. Metanoeó* means "to change one's mind, i.e. to repent; to change one's mind for the better, heartily to amend with abhorrence of one's past sins."[8]

True repentance means a change of heart about the sin you have committed—seeing it the way God sees it, renouncing it, and turning away from it. Paul the apostle broke it down scripturally and contrasted worldly sorry with godly sorrow in a powerful way in 2 Corinthians 7:8–12 (NKJV):

> For even if I made you sorry with my letter, I do not regret it; though I did regret it. For I perceive that the same epistle made you sorry, though only for a while. Now I rejoice, not that you were made sorry, but that your sorrow led to repentance. For you were made sorry in a godly manner, that you might suffer loss from us in nothing. For godly sorrow produces repentance leading to salvation, not to be regretted; but the sorrow of the world produces death. For observe this very thing, that you sorrowed in a godly manner: What diligence it produced in you, what clearing of yourselves, what indignation, what fear, what vehement desire, what zeal, what vindication! In all things you proved yourselves to be clear in this matter. Therefore, although I wrote to you, I did not do it for the sake of him who had done the wrong, nor for the sake of him who suffered wrong, but that our care for you in the sight of God might appear to you.

Charles Finney, one of the key figures in the Second Great Awakening, said this:

> To one who truly repents, sin looks like a very different thing from what it does to him who has not repented. Instead of looking like a thing that is desirable or fascinating, it looks the very opposite, most [hateful] and detestable, and he is astonished at himself that he ever

> could have desired such a thing. Impenitent sinners may look at sin and see that it will ruin them, because God will punish them for it; but, after all, it appears in itself desirable; they love it; they roll it under their tongue. If it could end in happiness, they never would think of abandoning it. But to the [truly repentant person] it is different: he looks at his own conduct as perfectly hateful. He looks back upon it, and exclaims, "How hateful, how detestable, how worthy of hell, such and such a thing was in me!"[9]

Don't let this call to repentance offend you. Heed the warning and the good news of John, the apostle of love, in 1 John 1:5–10:

> This then is the message which we have heard from Him and declare to you: God is light, and in Him is no darkness at all. If we say that we have fellowship with Him, yet walk in darkness, we lie and do not practice the truth. But if we walk in the light as He is in the light, we have fellowship one with another, and the blood of Jesus Christ His Son cleanses us from all sin.
>
> If we say that we have no sin, we deceive ourselves, and the truth is not in us. If we confess our sins, He is faithful and just to forgive us our sins and cleanse us from all unrighteousness. If we say that we have not sinned, we make Him a liar and His word is not in us.

Addressing Corporate Sin

Both nations and the body of Christ have a corporate identity. We know that if one part of the body suffers, all parts suffer with it (1 Cor. 12:26). We know that Jesus is coming to "present Himself to a glorious church, not having spot, or wrinkle, or any such thing, but that it should be holy and without blemish" (Eph. 5:27). In his book *Healing America's Wounds*, John

Dawson wrote, "We are called to live out the biblical practice of identificational repentance, a neglected truth that opens the floodgates of revival and brings healing to nations."[10]

There are plenty of examples of identificational repentance for corporate sin in the Old Testament. Moses, Daniel, Ezra, Nehemiah, and Jeremiah repented on behalf of their nation. Here are just a few of the many examples:

- **Moses made haste:** "Moses made haste and bowed to the ground and worshipped. He said, 'If now I have found favor in Your sight, O Lord, let my Lord, I pray, go among us, for we are a stiff-necked people. Pardon our iniquity and our sin, and take us for your inheritance'" (Exod. 34:8–9).
- **Daniel confessed sins:** "While I was speaking and praying and confessing my sin and the sin of my people Israel, and presenting my supplication before the LORD my God for the holy mountain of my God..." (Dan. 9:20).
- **Ezra was embarrassed:** "O my God, I am ashamed and embarrassed to lift up my face to You, my God, because our iniquities have expanded over our heads and our wrongdoing has grown up to the heavens. Since the days of our fathers until this day, we have been in a great guilt. It is because of our iniquities that we, our kings, and our priests have been delivered—by the sword, by captivity, by spoil, and by being shamed—into the hand of the kings of the lands. This day is like that, too" (Ezra 9:6–7). (This repentance continues through verse 15 if you want to read it in your Bible.)

- **Nehemiah cried out:** "Let Your ear now be attentive, and Your eyes open, that You may hear the prayer of Your servant, which I now pray before You, day and night, for the children of Israel Your servants, and confess the sins of the children of Israel, which we have sinned against You. Both my father's house and I have sinned" (Neh. 1:6).
- **Jeremiah was ashamed:** "We lie down in our shame, and our humiliation covers us. For we have sinned against the LORD our God, we and our fathers, from our youth even to this day, and have not obeyed the voice of the LORD our God" (Jer. 3:25).

So, practically, how do you make identificational repentance for corporate sin? While the examples of the prophets are strong, it starts with identifying the corporate sin. Although God does not demand that we necessarily go down a list, there are broad concepts like murder, sex trafficking, and drug abuse. When the Holy Spirit told me in 2007 that He would bring a third Great Awakening to America, He told me He required repentance for prayerlessness, abortion, and other broad categories of sin.

Once you have assessed the sin situation—both from your natural senses and from the Holy Spirit—you confess the sin and ask God for forgiveness. This is not a one-time effort since the sins are repeated over and over and there is no once and for all repentance. The key is to be led by the Spirit of God toward this corporate repentance. It must not be a rote exercise but a Spirit-inspired act of intercession. We keep doing it until it's over.

Part of repentance for corporate sin is pleading, or applying, the blood of Jesus. The blood of Jesus is sufficient for all sin—even the sin of a church, a city, or a nation. Finally, we need to do our part to repair the damage sin has done. That may mean, in some instances, going to repent to a people group, such as the Native Americans, in your region. In other cases it may mean performing a prophetic act. In still other cases it goes back to prophetic intercession that works to bring God's will and kingdom to bear.

Cleansing Generational Iniquity

Generational iniquity is another matter. Some Christians do not believe in generational curses—they feel every curse is broken with salvation. Although I agree that many people can be healed and set free instantly from addictions or disease at salvation, I have seen too many Christians break free from generational curses to believe that Christians cannot be cursed.

A generational curse is just what it sounds like: a curse that passes down from generation to generation. As Larry Huch, senior pastor of New Beginnings Church, told me, "The world says it like this, 'Like father like son.' The Word says it like this, 'The iniquity of the father passes on from generation to generation.'"[11] By the same token, Proverbs 26:2 says a curse without cause does not come any more than a bird accidently lands on a branch that holds its nest. We can inherit curses that block our blessings.

There are many passages in the Old Testament that explain how the Lord transfers the iniquity of the parents onto the children, including Exodus 20:5; 34:7; Leviticus 18:25; Numbers 14:8, 33; Deuteronomy 4:9; 7:10; Job 21:19; Psalms 79:8; 109:14–16; Isaiah 65:6–7; and Jeremiah 32:18. You can study these out, but let me leave you with one to ponder that demonstrates the curse and the blessing:

> You shall not bow down to them or serve them; for I, the LORD your God, am a jealous God, visiting the iniquity of the fathers on the children to the third and fourth generation of them who hate Me, and showing lovingkindness to thousands of them who love Me and keep My commandments.
>
> —EXODUS 20:5–6

So how do you discern a generational curse—and just as importantly, how do you break it? Look at the character traits in your family that are ungodly, such as rage, alcoholism, and divorce. Do you see negative patterns of sickness and disease in your bloodline? It could be more than bad DNA. It could be a generational curse. The most important action you can take is to pray and ask the Holy Spirit if there are generational curses in your life. You can break free.

"You can break it off yourself; you can break it off of your family members. The first step is to understand that Jesus died to forgive us of our sin so we can have every curse broken because 'cursed is everyone that hangs on a tree,'" Larry Huch told me. "Jesus redeemed us from the curse of the law with His blood on the cross. At the whipping post He took stripes and shed His blood again. By His stripes we are healed. But we just don't pray for people to be healed. We pray for the curse of disease to be broken by the blood of the Lamb."[12]

If you discern a generational curse operating in your life, here is a prayer you can say over yourself and your family: "Father, in the name of Jesus, I ask You to forgive me and the generations that have lived before me in my family line for every sin, iniquity, and transgression. I forgive every offense or wrong done against me and all those who have hurt me, and I ask You to bless them with Your love. I ask You to break every curse and every chain of bondage over my bloodline. I plead the blood of Jesus over myself and my family, and I ask You to help me align my thoughts and words with Your thoughts and Your Word. I thank You for the purifying power of Your blood, which cleanses me and my family line from all unrighteousness, and I ask You to help me to walk in obedience to Your will all the days of my life."

Standing in the Gap

God told Ezekiel He was looking for a man to stand in the gap for the land so He would not destroy it. I believe God is still looking for men and women—and even children—who will stand in the gap for people, churches, cities, states, and nations. Let's look at this scripture:

> I sought for a man among them who would build up the hedge and stand in the gap before Me for the land so that I would not destroy it, but I found no one. Therefore I have poured out My indignation on them. I have consumed them with the fire of My wrath. Their own way I have recompensed on their heads, says the Lord God.
>
> —Ezekiel 22:30–31

What did God want? He wanted an intercessor who would build up a hedge against the enemy. The Hebrew word for *hedge* in that verse is *gader*, which means "fence or wall."[13] As Matthew Henry's commentary explains, "Sin makes a gap in the hedge of protection that is about a people at which good things run out from them and evil things pour in upon them, a gap by which God enters to destroy them."[14] That is an intense thought—and here is an even more intense truth: intercessors who are called to make up a hedge and neglect to do so suffer the same fate as the rest.

God wanted an intercessor to stand in the gap. The Hebrew word for *gap* in this passage is *perets*, which means a "breach, gap, bursting forth," or a "broken wall."[15] Henry writes, "There is a way of standing in the gap, and making up the breach against the judgments of God, by repentance, and prayer, and reformation...When God is coming forth against a sinful people to destroy them he expects some to intercede for them, and enquires if there be but one that does; so much is it his desire and delight to show mercy. If there be but a man that stands in the gap, as Abraham for Sodom, he will discover him and be well pleased with him."[16]

God wants someone to wage prophetic warfare with repentance. He wants people who will grieve over the moral condition of a person, a family, or a nation, and respond to His call to intercession rooted in repentance for sin. God wants to forgive and to heal the land—but He cannot forgive sin without repentance.

Watching God Heal the Land

Once you have repented of the sins that hold back transforming revival, you can continue making intercession until the dynamics are set in place for God to heal the land. God has done it over and again. The Sentinel Group, a Christian research information agency dedicated to helping the church pray knowledgeably for end-time global evangelization and enabling communities to discover the pathway to genuine revival and societal transformation, has documented transformation in about one thousand communities worldwide.

One of these communities was Cali, Colombia, a city once known as the cocaine capital of the world. This reputation was certainly earned. The ruling drug cartel's power was widespread, and corruption was prevalent. However, God turned this city around when Christians, in their desperation for

God to move, began holding hours-long prayer vigils in local stadiums.[17]

Another example is Karawa. The locals in the village, located in Papua New Guinea, had long held a tradition of worshipping the devil. However, the people of the city recently showed deep remorse and repentance by burning their fetishes. Soon after these actions were taken, life improved dramatically—"salty water turned fresh, gardens thrived and abundant sealife returned."[18]

A final example is Fischer Village, Brazil. This little village has made huge steps forward in the last few years. Until recently most people in the town were living in a garbage dump. Living there was beyond difficult, and death and disease were widespread within the community. God heard their cries and turned their city around, bringing "dramatic healings, new homes, and fresh hope."[19]

True transformation is not based on man's opinion. Scripture offers evidence of indicators that are clearly visible. I offer more about this reality in my book *The Next Great Move of God: An Appeal to Heaven for Spiritual Awakening.*

Are you ready to run to the battle line? Remember, press in to get God's prophetic warfare strategy before you pick up your sword and start fighting. There are many methods and many tactics that God may reveal to you—and the one He reveals to you will lead you into ultimate victory, in the name of Jesus!

WHERE DO YOU GO FROM HERE?

THIS BOOK OFFERS thirteen prophetic warfare strategies that are proven to work—if you use the right one at the right time. Think about it this way: Your prophetic warfare arsenal is full of these tools. Just as a home builder would use one tool for laying the foundation and another tool for putting on the roof, you will learn by practical experience—and always with the leading of the Holy Spirit—when to use which prophetic warfare strategy in battle.

Many times the Holy Spirit will lead you to start off into intercession, which becomes prophetic intercession as He breathes on it. During this prophetic intercession, you may also pray in the Spirit, and a word of knowledge or prophecy may bubble up in your spirit. You may then transition to waging warfare with the prophetic word or taking faith-inspired action in your community, like a doing a prayer walk or prophetic act. Here we see the prophetic warfare strategies become building blocks that lead you to greater revelation and specific actions.

You may be a dreamer and receive prophetic revelation while you sleep. When you arise, you may begin to decree and declare what the Lord showed you in the dream, and that may send you into travail. You may be a spiritual mapper who roots out the sin in the land and calls upon local churches to engage in warfare repentance. Or you may discover that the

Lord reveals His strategies to you during times of praise and worship.

The point is that there is probably a way the Lord speaks to you most often—and that is how He will often share the prophetic warfare strategy. That said, be open to the Lord moving in new ways in your life. You can't just decide to go into travail, for example, but you can decide not to quench the burden for intercession when He lays it upon you. You can't decide to have a vision, but you can record the details if you do have one, and pray it through. It won't bear much fruit for you to do a march, prayer walk, or some prophetic act if the Holy Spirit is not the one who inspired it—but you can obey His leading even when it seems impossible, sounds strange, or makes no sense to your natural mind.

So where do you go from here? Walk in the Spirit, fellowship with Him, and keep the lines of communication open when you are in warfare and when you are not. When we cultivate intimacy with the Lord, many times He will show us what the enemy has planned and give us the strategy to thwart it before it manifests.

NOTES

Chapter 1—Calling All Prophetic Warriors

1. *Merriam-Webster Online*, s.v. "technology," accessed February 11, 2016, http://www.merriam-webster.com/dictionary/technology.

2. Ibid.

3. "Special Forces," Special Operations Recruiting Battalion (Airborne), last modified September 11, 2015, accessed February 11, 2016, http://www.sorbrecruiting.com/sf.htm.

4. *Merriam-Webster Online*, s.v. "technology."

5. Christine Ammer, *The American Heritage Dictionary of Idioms*, 2nd ed. (Boston: Houghton Mifflin Harcourt, 2013), 55.

6. Paul Heacock, ed., *Cambridge Dictionary of American Idioms* (Cambridge: Cambridge University Press, 2003), 332.

Chapter 2—Wielding the Weapons of Our Warfare

1. Thayer and Smith, *The KJV New Testament Greek Lexicon*, s.v. "*pale*," accessed February 12, 2016, http://www.biblestudytools.com/lexicons/greek/kjv/pale.html.

2. *Merriam-Webster Online*, s.v. "stranglehold," accessed February 11, 2016, http://www.merriam-webster.com/dictionary/stranglehold.

3. Thayer and Smith, *The KJV New Testament Greek Lexicon*, s.v. "*arche*," accessed February 12, 2016, http://www.biblestudytools.com/lexicons/greek/kjv/arche.html.

4. W. E. Vine, Merrill F. Unger, and William White Jr., *Vine's Complete Expository Dictionary of Old and New Testament Words*, 1940, accessed February 12, 2016, http://www.ultimatebiblereferencelibrary.com/Vines_Expositary_Dictionary.pdf.

5. Thayer and Smith, *The NAS New Testament Greek Lexicon*, s.v. "*exousia*," 1999, accessed February 12, 2016, http://www.biblestudytools.com/lexicons/greek/nas/exousia.html.

6. Ibid., s.v. "*kosmokrator*," accessed February 12, 2016, http://www.biblestudytools.com/lexicons/greek/nas/kosmokrator.html.

7. Thayer and Smith, *The KJV New Testament Greek Lexicon*, s.v. "*poneria*," accessed February 12, 2016, http://www.biblestudytools.com/lexicons/greek/kjv/poneria.html.

8. Ibid., s.v. "*hoplon*," accessed February 12, 2016, http://www.biblestudytools.com/lexicons/greek/kjv/hoplon.html.

9. Ibid., s.v. "*strateia*," accessed February 12, 2016, http://www.biblestudytools.com/lexicons/greek/kjv/strateia.html.

10. Ibid.

11. Ibid., s.v. "*sarkikos*," accessed February 12, 2016, http://www.biblestudytools.com/lexicons/greek/kjv/sarkikos.html.

12. Thayer and Smith, *The NAS New Testament Greek Lexicon*, s.v. "*dunatos*," accessed February 12, 2016, http://www.biblestudytools.com/lexicons/greek/nas/dunatos.html.

Chapter 3—The Art and Science of Prophetic Intercession

1. Cindy Jacobs, *The Voice of God: How God Speaks Personally and Corporately to His Children Today* (Ventura, CA: Regal Books, 1995), 39.

2. James W. Goll, "An Urgent Call to Prophetic Intercession," *Charisma*, December 8, 2014, http://www.charismamag.com/blogs/a-voice-calling-out/21975-an-urgent-call-to-prophetic-intercession.

3. Ibid.

4. Ibid.

5. Dutch Sheets, foreword to *Prophetic Intercession*, by Barbara Wentroble (Ventura, CA: Regal Books, 1999), 14.

6. *Merriam-Webster Online*, s.v. "despondent," accessed February 12, 2016, http://www.merriam-webster.com/dictionary/despondent.

7. Heart of the Prophetic's Facebook page, Jennifer LeClaire, November 21, 2014, accessed February 12, 2016, https://www.facebook.com/propheticbooks/posts/10152917551914040.

8. E. M. Bounds, *The Reality of Prayer* (Grand Rapids, MI: Christian Classics Ethereal Library), 64, accessed February 12, 2016, http://www.ccel.org/ccel/bounds/reality.pdf.

9. E. M. Bounds, *The Complete Works of E. M. Bounds on Prayer: Experience the Wonders of God Through Prayer* (Grand Rapids, MI: Baker Books, 2013).

10. Heart of the Prophetic's Facebook page, Jennifer LeClaire, November 21, 2014, accessed February 12, 2016, https://www.facebook.com/propheticbooks/posts/10152917551914040.

Chapter 4—Praying in the Spirit

1. Thayer and Smith, *The KJV New Testament Greek Lexicon*, s.v. "*sunantilambanomai*," accessed February 16, 2016, http://www.biblestudytools.com/lexicons/greek/kjv/sunantilambanomai.html.

2. Thayer and Smith, *The NAS New Testament Greek Lexicon*, s.v. "*astheneia*," accessed February 16, 2016, http://www.biblestudytools.com/lexicons/greek/nas/astheneia.html.

3. Thayer and Smith, *The KJV New Testament Greek Lexicon*, s.v. "*musterion*," accessed February 16, 2016, http://www.biblestudytools.com/lexicons/greek/kjv/musterion.html.

4. Bill Hamon, "Why Speaking in Tongues Matters," *Charisma*, August 22, 2013, http://www.charismamag.com/spirit/supernatural/11538-evidence-of-the-gift.

5. *Merriam-Webster Online*, s.v. "mystery," accessed February 16, 2016, http://www.merriam-webster.com/dictionary/mystery.

6. Thayer and Smith, *The KJV New Testament Greek Lexicon*, s.v. "*sophia*," accessed February 16, 2016, http://www.biblestudytools.com/lexicons/greek/kjv/sophia.html.

7. Larry Sparks, "5 Ways That Praying in Tongues Will Change Your Life Forever," *Charisma*, March 23, 2014, http://www.charismanews.com/opinion/43206-5-ways-that-praying-in-tongues-will-change-your-life-forever.

8. Ibid.

9. "America's Best Weapon: Patience," *New York Times*, October 21, 1990, http://www.nytimes.com/1990/10/21/opinion/america-s-best-weapon-patience.html.

Chapter 5—Prophetic Dreams That Unlock Spiritual Warfare Strategies

1. *Merriam-Webster Online*, s.v. "dream," accessed February 16, 2016, http://www.merriam-webster.com/dictionary/dream.

2. Francis Brown, S. R. Driver, Charles A. Briggs, and Wilhelm Gesenius, *The KJV Old Testament Hebrew Lexicon*, s.v. "*chalown*," accessed February 16, 2016, http://www.biblestudytools.com/lexicons/hebrew/kjv/chalowm.html.

3. Thayer and Smith, *The KJV New Testament Greek Lexicon*, s.v. "*enupniazomai*," accessed February 16, 2016, http://www.biblestudytools.com/lexicons/greek/kjv/enupniazomai.html.

4. Rick Joyner, as quoted in Jennifer LeClaire, "The Only Way to Defeat the Behemoth of Islam," *Charisma*, December 1, 2014, http://www.charismanews.com/opinion/46307-the-only-way-to-defeat-the-behemoth-of-islam.

Chapter 6—Seeing Warfare Tactics in Prophetic Visions

1. Jennifer LeClaire, "When a Vision of Raising the Dead Becomes Reality," JenniferLeclaire.org, accessed May 12, 2016, http://www

.jenniferleclaire.org/articles/when-a-vision-of-raising-the-dead-becomes-reality.

2. Ibid.
3. Ibid.
4. Ibid.
5. Ibid.

Chapter 7—The Power of Prophetic Declarations, Decrees, and Proclamations

1. "The Virginia Stamp Act Resolutions—1765," USHistory.org, accessed February 16, 2016, http://www.ushistory.org/declaration/related/vsa65.html.

2. "Proclamation—America Seeks God in a Time of War—1777," WallBuilders.com, accessed February 16, 2016, http://www.wallbuilders.com/libissuesarticles.asp?id=56.

3. *Merriam-Webster Online*, s.v. "decree," accessed February 19, 2016, http://www.merriam-webster.com/dictionary/decree.

4. Ibid., s.v. "declare," accessed February 19, 2016, http://www.merriam-webster.com/dictionary/declare.

5. Ibid., s.v. "declaration," accessed February 19, 2016, http://www.merriam-webster.com/dictionary/declaration.

6. Ibid., s.v. "proclaim," accessed February 22, 2016, http://www.merriam-webster.com/dictionary/proclaim.

7. Ibid., s.v. "proclamation," accessed February 22, 2016, http://www.merriam-webster.com/dictionary/proclamation.

8. "Proclamation—America Seeks God in a Time of War—1777," WallBuilders.com, accessed February 16, 2016, http://www.wallbuilders.com/libissuesarticles.asp?id=56; *Journals of the American Congress from 1774 to 1788* (Washington: Way and Gideon, 1823), Vol. II, 309–310.

Chapter 8—Executing Spirit-Inspired Prophetic Acts

1. "Window Rock," VisitArizona.com, accessed February 22, 2016, http://www.visitarizona.com/places-to-visit/northern-arizona/window-rock.

2. Harrison Lapahie Jr., "Window Rock," Lapahie.com, accessed February 22, 2016, http://www.lapahie.com/window_rock_capitol.cfm.

3. "Navajo Water Project," Navajo Water Project, DigDeep, accessed February 22, 2016, http://www.navajowaterproject.org/project-specifics/.

4. Centers for Disease Control and Prevention, "Suicide Among Adults Aged 35–64 Years—United States, 1999–2010," *Weekly* 62, no.

17 (May 3, 2013): 321–325, http://www.cdc.gov/mmwr/preview/mmwrhtml/mm6217a1.htm?s_cid=mm6217a1_w.

5. "Tribal Communities," The United States Department of Justice, last modified December 14, 2015, accessed February 22, 2016, http://www.justice.gov/ovw/tribal-communities.

6. "Navajo Nation Launches Nationwide Search for Police Chief," Daily Mail.com, January 23, 2016, accessed April 14, 2016, http://www.dailymail.co.uk/wires/ap/article-3413186/Navajo-Nation-launches-nationwide-search-police-chief.html.

7. Danika Worthington, "Navajo Nation Schools Receive $45M in Overdue Federal Funding," AZCentral.com, January 15, 2016, accessed April 14, 2016, http://www.azcentral.com/story/news/local/arizona/2016/01/15/navajo-nation-schools-receive-45m-overdue-federal-funding/78845968/.

8. Stephanie Van Dyke, "Wholesome Wave and Navajo Nation Partner to Overcome Food Insecurity in Navajo Nation," Foodtank.com, January 11, 2016, accessed April 14, 2016, http://foodtank.com/news/2016/01/Wholesome-Wave-and-Navajo-Nation-Healthy-Food-Access.

9. Steven Nelson, "Judge Found Guilty of Corruption Gets $25 Fine," US News, March 7, 2016, accessed April 14, 2016, http://www.usnews.com/news/articles/2016-03-07/judge-found-guilty-of-corruption-gets-25-fine.

10. "Carter Ledyard Represents Keybanc Capital Markets in Historic $53 Million Bond Issuance by the Navajo Nation," Carter Ledyard & Milburn, accessed April 14, 2016, http://www.clm.com/news item.cfm?ID=3687.

11. Dutch Sheets, *Intercessory Prayer: How God Can Use Your Prayers to Move Heaven and Earth* (Ventura, CA: Regal Books, 1996), 232.

12. Barbara Wentroble, *Prophetic Intercession: Letting God Lead Your Prayers* (Bloomington, MN: Chosen Books, 1999), 113.

13. Chuck Pierce, *The Future War of the Church: How We Can Defeat Lawlessness and Bring God's Order to Earth* (Ventura, CA: Regal Books, 2007), 37.

14. Jacobs, *The Voice of God*, 43.

15. "Exodus 17," *Matthew Henry Commentary on the Whole Bible (Complete)*, accessed February 12, 2016, http://www.biblestudytools.com/commentaries/matthew-henry-complete/exodus/17.html.

16. Dutch Sheets, "Isaiah 22:22: The Key to Governmental Authority," Dutch Sheets Ministries, December 30, 2014, http://www.dutchsheets.org/isaiah-2222-the-key-to-governmental-authority/.

Chapter 9—Waging War With Prophetic Words

1. "Extreme Prophetic Studies: All Can Prophesy," JonasClark.com, accessed April 22, 2016, http://www.jonasclark.com/bibleschool/course/data/reading/LESSON%202%20ALL%20CAN%20PROPHESY.pdf.
2. Ibid.
3. Ibid.
4. Joyce Meyer Ministries Facebook page, October 24, 2013, accessed February 23, 2016, https://www.facebook.com/joycemeyerministries/posts/10151947385552384.

Chapter 10—Pressing Into Throne Room Praise and Worship

1. Thayer and Smith, *The KJV New Testament Greek Lexicon*, s.v. "*soteria*," accessed February 23, 2016, http://www.biblestudytools.com/lexicons/greek/kjv/soteria.html.
2. Brown, Driver, Briggs, and Gesenius, *The KJV Old Testament Hebrew Lexicon*, s.v. "*berekah*," accessed February 23, 2016, http://www.biblestudytools.com/lexicons/hebrew/kjv/berakah-2.html.
3. Nicole Hensley, "Ten-Year-Old Sings Gospel Song to Overcome Kidnapper in Atlanta," *New York Daily News*, April 18, 2014, http://www.nydailynews.com/news/national/10-year-old-sings-gospel-song-defeat-ga-kidnapper-article-1.1761282.
4. Blayne Alexander, "Boy's Love of Gospel Music May Have Saved His Life," 11alive.com, April 23, 2014, http://www.11alive.com/story/news/local/southwest-atlanta/2014/04/17/willie-myrick-gospel-kidnapping/7851279/.
5. Ibid.
6. Ibid.
7. Ibid.
8. Thayer and Smith, *The KJV New Testament Greek Lexicon*, s.v. "*seismos*," accessed February 23, 2016, http://www.biblestudytools.com/lexicons/greek/kjv/seismos.html.

Chapter 11—Tapping Into the Prophetic Power of Travail

1. Thayer and Smith, *The KJV New Testament Greek Lexicon*, s.v. "*stenagmos*," accessed February 23, 2016, http://www.biblestudytools.com/lexicons/greek/kjv/stenagmos.html.

2. *Merriam-Webster Online*, s.v. "travail," accessed February 23, 2016, http://www.merriam-webster.com/dictionary/travail.

3. *Webster's Revised Unabridged Dictionary* (Springfield, MA: C. & G. Merriam Co., 1913), s.v. "travail."

4. James W. Goll, *The Prophetic Intercessor: Releasing God's Purposes to Change Lives and Influence Nations* (Grand Rapids, MI: Chosen Books, 2007), 67.

5. Barbara Yoder, as quoted in Chuck Pierce, "A Time to Travail: Moving from Distress to Victory," GloryofZion.org, March 12, 2007, accessed February 24, 2016, https://www.gloryofzion.org/outmail/3-12-07_A_TimeToTravailOnline.htm.

6. Thayer and Smith, *The KJV New Testament Greek Lexicon*, s.v. "*tikto*," accessed February 24, 2016, http://www.biblestudytools.com/lexicons/greek/kjv/tikto.html.

7. Ibid., s.v. "*mochthos*," accessed February 24, 2016, http://www.biblestudytools.com/lexicons/greek/kjv/mochthos.html.

8. Brown, Driver, Briggs, and Gesenius, *The KJV Old Testament Hebrew Lexicon*, s.v. "*yalad*," accessed February 24, 2016, http://www.biblestudytools.com/lexicons/hebrew/kjv/yalad.html.

9. Ibid., s.v. "*tĕla'ah*," accessed February 24, 2016, http://www.biblestudytools.com/lexicons/hebrew/kjv/telaah.html.

10. Ibid., s.v. "*`inyan*," accessed February 24, 2016, http://www.biblestudytools.com/lexicons/hebrew/kjv/inyan.html.

11. Brown, Drive, Briggs, and Gesenius, *The NAS Old Testament Hebrew Lexicon*, s.v. "*chalah*," accessed May 10, 2016, http://www.biblestudytools.com/lexicons/hebrew/nas/chalah.html.

12. Brown, Driver, Briggs, and Gesenius, *The KJV Old Testament Hebrew Lexicon*, s.v. "*`amal*," accessed February 24, 2016, http://www.biblestudytools.com/lexicons/hebrew/kjv/amal-3.html.

13. Cindy Jacobs, *Possessing the Gates of the Enemy: A Training Manual for Militant Intercession* (Grand Rapids, MI: Chosen, 2009), 110.

14. Ibid.

15. Brown, Driver, Briggs and Gesenius, *The KJV Old Testament Hebrew Lexicon*, s.v. "*ruwa`*," accessed February 24, 2016, http://www.biblestudytools.com/lexicons/hebrew/kjv/ruwa.html.

16. Ibid.

17. Ibid., s.v. "*pa'ah`*," accessed February 24, 2016, http://www.biblestudytools.com/lexicons/hebrew/kjv/paah-2.html.

18. James Goll, "Travail: The Prayer That Brings Birth," The Elijah List, January 21, 2005, accessed February 24, 2016, http://www.elijahlist.com/words/display_word/2791.

19. Jacobs, *Possessing the Gates*, 111.

20. Chuck Pierce, "A Time to Travail: Moving From Distress to Victory," GloryofZion.org, March 12, 2007, accessed February 24, 2016, https://www.gloryofzion.org/outmail/3-12-07_A_TimeToTravailOnline.htm.

Chapter 12—Partnering With Angelic Warriors

1. James Strong, *The New Strong's Expanded Exhaustive Concordance of the Bible* (Nashville: Thomas Nelson, 2001), s.v. "principalities."

2. *Merriam-Webster Online*, s.v. "principality," accessed February 24, 2016, http://www.merriam-webster.com/dictionary/principality.

3. *Strong's Concordance*, s.v. "*exousia*," accessed April 19, 2016, http://biblehub.com/greek/1849.htm.

4. Ibid., s.v. "*ponéria*," accessed April 19, 2016, http://biblehub.com/greek/4189.htm; *Strong's Exhaustive Concordance*, http://biblehub.com/greek/4189.htm.

5. *Merriam-Webster Online*, s.v. "malice," accessed February 24, 2016, http://www.merriam-webster.com/dictionary/malice.

6. Thayer and Smith, *The KJV New Testament Greek Lexicon*, s.v. "*kosmokrator*," accessed February 24, 2016, http://www.biblestudytools.com/lexicons/greek/kjv/kosmokrator.html.

7. Ibid., s.v. "*skotos*," accessed February 24, 2016, http://www.biblestudytools.com/lexicons/greek/kjv/skotos.html.

8. Lester Sumrall, *Angels to Help You* (New Kensington, PA: Whitaker House, 1982).

Chapter 13—Spiritual Mapping That Releases Prophetic Plans

1. *Merriam-Webster Online*, s.v. "map," accessed February 25, 2016, http://www.merriam-webster.com/dictionary/map.

2. George Otis Jr., *The Last of the Giants: Lifting the Veil on Islam and the End Times* (Ada, MI: Chosen Books, 1991), 85.

3. In communication with the author.

4. C. Peter Wagner, *Breaking Spiritual Strongholds in Your City* (Shippensburg, PA: Destiny Image, 2015). Viewed at Google Books.

5. Nickson Banda, *Dynamics of Spiritual Warfare: Biblical Foundations for Waging Spiritual Battles and for Arresting Demonic Forces* (Bloomington, IN: AuthorHouse, 2010), 51.

6. Cindy Jacobs, "How to Prophetically Lay Siege to a City," *Charisma*, accessed February 25, 2016, http://www.charismamag.com/spirit/devotionals/loving-god?view=article&id=18483:how-to-prophetically-lay-siege-to-a-city&catid=1567.

7. "LGBT Populations," LGBTMap.org, accessed February 25, 2016, http://www.lgbtmap.org/equality-maps/lgbt_populations.

8. "Florida State: Crime," BestPlaces.net, accessed February 25, 2016, http://www.bestplaces.net/crime/state/florida.

9. "Florida Crossroads—Cassadaga: Psychic Capital of the World," The Florida Channel, October 28, 2013, accessed May 10, 2016, http://thefloridachannel.org/videos/cassadaga-psychic-capital-of-the-world/.

10. "NeighborhoodScout's Most Dangerous Cities—2016: Top 100 Most Dangerous Cities in the U.S.," NeighborhoodScout.com, accessed February 25, 2016, http://www.neighborhoodscout.com/neighborhoods/crime-rates/top100dangerous/.

11. Claire McNeill, "Florida Seeing Highest Number of New HIV Cases in the Nation," *Tampa Bay Times*, July 2, 2015, accessed April 14, 2016, http://www.tampabay.com/news/health/new-hiv-infections-in-hillsborough-county-highest-in-the-state/2236007.

12. Jennifer LeClaire, "Why Are So Many Pastors Committing Suicide?" *Charisma*, December 11, 2013, http://www.charismanews.com/opinion/watchman-on-the-wall/42063-why-are-so-many-pastors-committing-suicide; Jennifer LeClaire, "Why Megachurch Pastors Keep Falling Into Sexual Immorality," *Charisma*, May 8, 2013, http://www.charismanews.com/opinion/39397-why-megachurch-pastors-keep-falling-into-sexual-immorality.

13. John Dawson, *Taking Our Cities for God: How to Break Spiritual Strongholds* (Lake Mary, FL: Charisma House, 2001), 58–59.

14. "Nateleira, Fiji," The Sentinel Group, September 4, 2013, accessed June 30, 2016, http://www.journeytotransformation.com/nateleira-fiji/.

15. In communication with the author.

Chapter 14—Prophetic Prayer Walks and Marches

1. Jack Kelley, "New 'Cash Crop' in Ky.; Pot 'Revitalizes' Clay Co.; 4 out of 10 in County Said to Grow Weed," *USA Today*, July 11, 1989, Final Edition.

2. "Special Report: Prescription for Pain," *Lexington Herald-Leader*, January–February 2003, accessed December 15, 2014, http://operationunite.org/wp-content/uploads/2010/06/Prescription-For-Pain-Part1-copy.pdf.

3. Jennifer LeClaire, "A Heavenly Appeal: Prophetic Leaders Bombard God's Throne," *Charisma*, May 2015, http://www.charismamag.com/spirit/revival/23059-an-appeal-to-heaven.

4. Ibid.

5. Ibid.

6. Ibid.

7. Wendy Griffith, "Town's Radical Change a 'Hope for America,'" CBN News, October 22, 2010, accessed February 26, 2016, http://www.cbn.com/cbnnews/us/2010/october/appalachia-towns-transformation-a-hope-for-america-/?mobile=false; Beth Smith, "Speaker Tells Officers How Churches Helped Town in Drug Spiral," *Evansville Courier and Press*, May 19, 2011, http://www.courierpress.com/news/speaker-tells-officers-how-churches-helped-town-in-drug-spiral-ep-445518772-324962141.html.

8. LeClaire, "A Heavenly Appeal."

9. Brown, Driver, Briggs, and Gesenius, *The KJV Old Testament Hebrew Lexicon*, s.v. "*charash*," accessed February 26, 2016, http://www.biblestudytools.com/lexicons/hebrew/kjv/charash.html.

10. Steve Hawthorne and Graham Kendrick, *Prayerwalking: Praying On Site With Insight* (Lake Mary, FL: Charisma House, 1993), 12.

11. Ibid., 13.

12. Ibid.

13. Ibid.

14. Steve Weber, "Stories of Gumption—Lyn Hanush," SpeakingGump.com, February 11, 2011, accessed April 14, 2016, http://speakinggump.com/blog/stories-of-gumption-lyn-hanush/.

15. "About Lyn," GreatAmericanJourney.com, accessed February 26, 2016, http://greatamericanjourney.com/about/; "Woman Prayer-Walks the United States," CBN.com, video, accessed February 26, 2016, http://www1.cbn.com/content/woman-prayer-walks-united-states-0.

Chapter 15—When Repentance Is Warfare

1. John Dawson, *Healing America's Wounds: Discovering Our Destiny* (Ventura, CA: Regal Books, 1994).

2. *Oxford Dictionaries Online*, s.v. "identificational," accessed February 26, 2016, http://www.oxforddictionaries.com/us/definition/american_english/identificational.

3. Ibid., s.v. "identification," accessed February 26, 2016, http://www.oxforddictionaries.com/us/definition/american_english/identification.

4. C. Peter Wagner, *Praying with Power* (Shippensburg, PA: Destiny Image, 1997); C. Peter Wagner, as quoted in Geoff Waugh, "The Power to Heal the Past," Renewal Journal (blog), July 18, 2011, https://renewaljournal.wordpress.com/2011/07/18/the-power-to-heal-the-past-by-c-peter-wagner/.

5. "The Order for the Visitation of the Sick," The Church of England, accessed April 14, 2016, https://www.churchofengland.org/prayer-worship/worship/book-of-common-prayer/the-visitation-of-the-sick.aspx.

6. "History: Timeline," EpiscopalChurch.org, accessed February 26, 2016, http://www.episcopalchurch.org/page/history-timeline.

7. *The Book of Occasional Services: 2003* (New York: Church Publishing, 2004), 66.

8. Thayer's Greek Lexicon, s.v. "*metanoeó*,"accessed April 19, 2016, http://biblehub.com/greek/3340.htm.

9. H. D. M. Spence, Joseph S. Exell, and Charles Neil, eds., *Christian Dogmatics* (New York: Funk and Wagnalls, 1889), 366.

10. Dawson, *Healing America's Wounds*, 30.

11. Jennifer LeClaire, "My Interview with Pastor Larry Huch on Breaking Generational Curses," Jennifer LeClaire Ministries, accessed May 11, 2016, http://www.jenniferleclaire.org/articles/my_interview_with_pastor_larry_huch_on_breaking_generational_curses.

12. Ibid.

13. Brown, Driver, Briggs, and Gesenius, *The KJV Old Testament Hebrew Lexicon*, s.v. "*gader*," accessed February 26, 2016, http://www.biblestudytools.com/lexicons/hebrew/kjv/gader.html.

14. *Matthew Henry Commentary on the Whole Bible*, accessed February 26, 2016, http://www.biblestudytools.com/commentaries/matthew-henry-complete/ezekiel/22.html.

15. Brown, Driver, Briggs, and Gesenius, *The KJV Old Testament Hebrew Lexicon*, s.v. "*perets*," accessed February 26, 2016, http://www.biblestudytools.com/lexicons/hebrew/kjv/perets.html.

16. *Matthew Henry Commentary on the Whole Bible*, accessed February 26, 2016, http://www.biblestudytools.com/commentaries/matthew-henry-complete/ezekiel/22.html.

17. "Cali, Colombia," The Sentinel Group, September 4, 2013, accessed June 30, 2016, http://www.journeytotransformation.com/cali-colombia/.

18. "Karawu, Papua New Guinea," The Sentinel Group, September 4, 2013, accessed June 30, 2016, http://www.journeytotransformation.com/karawu-papua-new-guinea/.

19. "Fischer Village, Brazil," The Sentinel Group, September 4, 2013, accessed June 30, 2016, http://www.journeytotransformation.com/fischer-village-brazil/.